Amazon Bestselling Author of
The Chausathi Yoginis of Hirapur and The Yoginis of Ranipur Jharial

Hidden Heritage: The Lesser-Known Temples of Odisha

Hidden Heritage:
The Lesser-Known Temples of Odisha

Dr. Adyasha Das

BLACK EAGLE BOOKS
Dublin, USA | Bhubaneswar, India

Black Eagle Books
USA address:
7464 Wisdom Lane
Dublin, OH 43016

India address:
E/312, Trident Galaxy, Kalinga Nagar,
Bhubaneswar-751003, Odisha, India

E-mail: info@blackeaglebooks.org
Website: www.blackeaglebooks.org

First International Edition Published by
Black Eagle Books, 2025

**HIDDEN HERITAGE: THE LESSER-KNOWN
TEMPLES OF ODISHA**
by **Dr. Adyasha Das**

Copyright © Dr. Adyasha Das

All rights reserved. No part of this publication may be reproduced, stored in a retrieval system, or transmitted, in any form or by any means, electronic, mechanical, photocopying, recording or otherwise without the prior permission of the publisher.

Cover & Interior Design: Ezy's Publication

ISBN- 978-1-64560-644-4 (Paperback)
Library of Congress Control Number: 2025931131

Printed in the United States of America

To the sacred presence that dwells within ancient temples, whispering timeless tales—this book is a tribute to the spirit that endures, unseen yet eternal.

Contents

Preface	09
Gangeswari Temple	19
Pataleswara Temple	27
Barahi Temple	31
Madhab Temple	38
Sobhaneswar Temple	46
Swapneswar Temple	53
Gajasimha Mandap	59
Amuhan Deula	64
Tipuri Hero-Stones	67
Bimala Temple	70
DakshinaKali Temple	75
Indralath Temple	82
Pataneswari Temple	86
Kechela Jain Idols	93
Twin Temples of Gandharadi	98
Batrish Singhasan	103
Subei Jain temple	106
Ambika Temple	112
Raghunath Temple	117
Narasimha Temple	121
Puri Varahi Temple	124
Gateswar Temple	127
Bedhakali Temple	130
Shyamakali Temple	136
Leharigudi Temple	140
Someswar Temple	143
Lankeswari Temple	147
Temples of Mahendragiri	150
Murga Mahadev Temple	155
Tantra Temples	158

Preface

Indian heritage is a rich pot-pourri of diverse cultural, historical, and spiritual components. Heritage and its conservation and preservation have become increasingly important in the contemporary world, driven by their multifaceted benefits that extend beyond mere historical preservation. Heritage conservation helps preserve the history and traditions of a society, providing a sense of identity and connection for current and future generations. This is crucial for community building and strengthening social bonds within communities. Heritage sites and cultural artifacts are significant economic assets. They attract tourists, sustain livelihoods, and attract investment, thereby boosting local economies. The cultural industries

are key components of modern economies, and the prevalence of cultural sites and services can enhance the economic vitality of a region.

Among the many states that contribute to India's vibrant heritage, Odisha stands out for its unique blend of tangible and intangible cultural assets. Odisha, formerly known as Orissa, is a state in eastern India that boasts a long and uninterrupted history. The state's tangible heritage includes some of the most magnificent architectural marvels in India.

The cultural heritage of Odisha, both tangible and intangible, plays a significant role in promoting tourism and economic growth in the state. Odisha's cultural heritage is a treasure trove of historical, aesthetic, and spiritual significance. The state's tangible heritage, including its magnificent temples and monuments, and its intangible heritage, encompassing traditional art forms and festivals, make it a unique and enriching cultural destination. The economic and touristic value of this heritage underscores its importance for the state's development. Odisha offers to the scholars of history and temple architecture as well as to tourists a scope to study temples of amazing diversity, both well-known and lesser known. Both the aspects of evolution of temple architecture and the presence of variety in one place are unique in India.

The new- age visitor to temples goes in search of mindfulness. Mindfulness is a practice considered to be an integral part of various religious and secular traditions. It was practiced in the East by religious and spiritual institutions, while in the West its popularity was primarily due to particular people and secular institutions. The temples, considered to be the primary religious organizations, are changing roles to fit the new social trend.

In the past, temples were the centre of community lifestyles and religious activity.

The rich cultural and architectural heritage of Odisha is not confined to the well-known temples of popular pilgrimage sites. Scattered across its length and breadth are thousands of forgotten, at times nameless temples, standing as silent witnesses to its spiritual, architectural, and cultural legacy. These temples, often found in anonymous villages or rural parts of Odisha, have become overshadowed by time, neglect, and a lack of documentation. Despite their ruinous state, they represent both tangible and intangible heritage, encompassing the artistic mastery of ancient builders, the spiritual practices of forgotten communities, and the historical narratives that have shaped regions and cultures. The lesser-known temples of Odisha are remarkable examples of tangible heritage, representing the craftsmanship, architectural styles, and construction techniques of bygone eras. The stone carvings, intricate sculptures, and towering shikharas (spires) of these temples are evidence of the sophisticated temple-building practices prevalent in ancient Odisha. Despite their decay, the artistry and engineering skills embedded in these structures continue to command admiration.

Beyond their physical form, these temples embody Odisha's intangible heritage—spiritual practices, religious rituals, and cultural narratives. They are centres of worship, places where local communities gather to celebrate festivals, perform rituals, and pass down sacred traditions. Over time, these intangible aspects have faded, but the temples still resonate with the spiritual energy of the past. Oral traditions and folk rituals, often specific to the region, are tied to these temples, representing a blend of Vedic practices. Odisha's forgotten temples are treasures of both tangible and intangible heritage, silently holding within them the cultural, religious, and architectural legacy of the past. They are the heritage of ancient villages, dynasties, and communities whose stories have been forgotten; but physical remains still stand as evidence of their existence. Restoring these shrines is not only a means of preserving ancient art and architecture but also an essential step toward reclaiming our cultural identity and historical knowledge.

Having grown up in a family steeped in cultural traditions, my childhood was filled with visits to temples, which I cherished deeply. Little did I know that these early experiences would later inspire my research and lead me back to these sacred spaces. In my book, " The Sacred World of Temples," I explore my temple trails across India and various regions of South Asia. My fascination extends beyond the stunning architecture and intricate iconography; it is the profound, mindful connections I have formed with these sacred abodes that truly draw me in.

This book, "*Hidden Heritage: The Lesser-Known Temples of Odisha*" is an exploration of the rich and often overlooked ancient cultural heritage of Odisha. It is an attempt to shed light on numerous temples that, while lesser known, embody the state's historical depth and artistic achievements. The book emphasizes the importance of these temples as cultural landmarks that reflect the spiritual and historical narratives of Odisha. It highlights how each temple carries unique stories that contribute to the understanding of local traditions and community identities. It showcases the variety of architectural styles present in Odisha, particularly Kalinga architecture, which is characterized by intricate carvings and sculptures. The book discusses contemporary challenges in preserving these heritage sites, including neglect and environmental threats.

I have visited all the temples in course of my travels and research. Beyond their architectural beauty, the temples are portrayed as active places of worship that continue to play a vital role in the spiritual lives of local communities. The book invites readers to engage with these sites not just as historical artifacts but as living expressions of faith. *"Hidden Heritage: The Lesser-Known Temples of Odisha"* serves as both an informative guide and a passionate appeal for the recognition and preservation of Odisha's temple heritage. By illuminating these hidden gems, the book fosters a deeper appreciation for the diverse historical narratives that shape our world today.

In a state as culturally rich as Odisha, where ancient history and art have left their indelible imprints, it is both a responsibility and an honour to bring attention to its forgotten and lesser-known temples. Odisha's architectural marvels, like the famed Jagannath Temple of Puri and the Sun Temple of Konark, have captured global admiration. Yet, across the state, nestled in remote villages, hidden amid lush landscapes, or overshadowed by larger shrines, lie countless temples that are no less remarkable. These structures tell stories not just of deities and devotion, but of dynasties, artisanship, and the very soul of Odia culture.

In researching for this book, I found myself on a journey across time itself, wandering in the footprints of those who built and worshipped in these hallowed spaces. These temples hold narratives of centuries-old traditions, unique forms of architecture, and local legends that risk fading into oblivion if not documented and shared. These lesser-known temples are often unguarded treasures of art, with carvings that depict daily life, mythology, and folklore, preserving fragments of the past in ways no history book could capture.

Writing about these temples is a means to revive cultural memory and instil a renewed appreciation for Odisha's heritage. It is a call to reconnect with a part of our past that is slipping away—faded murals, broken idols, and inscriptions eroded by time yet filled with meaning. Through this book, I hope readers will sense the irreplaceable beauty in these forgotten spaces and feel a shared responsibility to protect them, not only as artifacts of the past but as living testimonies of an enduring legacy that belongs to every Odia, to every lover of history and art, and to humanity itself.

The Indian National Trust for Art and Cultural Heritage (INTACH) has been at the forefront of preserving India's rich cultural and architectural heritage, with a special focus on conserving ancient temples and other historical monuments. Founded in 1984, INTACH's mission is to safeguard India's diverse heritage, including its built, natural, and cultural legacy. The organization has undertaken numerous projects across the country to restore old temples, ensuring that these important symbols of India's past continue to inspire future generations. As the Co-convenor of Intach Bhubaneswar Chapter, I have benefitted hugely by joining hands for several initiatives towards heritage preservation and conservation. I am thankful to Shri Anil Dhir, Convenor, Intach Bhubaneswar Chapter and Deepak Kumar Nayak, Co-convenor, Intach Cuttack Chapter who have accompanied me for some of these drives and helped me with their insight and invaluable support.

I have designed heritage and cultural preservation activities through the Culture and Heritage Club at the Indian Institute of Tourism and Travel Management (IITTM) in Bhubaneswar. Our work focuses on promoting awareness and engagement in the preservation of Odisha's rich cultural heritage, particularly through community involvement and educational initiatives. We have undertaken various projects aimed at documenting and conserving ancient temples and archaeological sites in the region. The focus has been to integrate local communities into these efforts, fostering a sense of ownership and responsibility towards their cultural heritage. This approach not only aids in the preservation of historical sites but also enhances local tourism, contributing to the economic development of the area.

This book is an invite to readers to embark on a captivating journey of the *Hidden Heritage: Lesser-known Temples of Odisha* where the echoes of an ancient land whisper untold stories of a rich cultural fabric. It is a tribute to the resilience of a cultural legacy waiting to be rediscovered.

I thank Satya Pattanaik, Director, Black Eagle Books, USA for supporting the publication of this book. He has published my books previously and extended his unstinted support for their sustained promotion. Five of my books have made it to the Amazon Bestseller list. I thank Ashok Parida for his efforts towards the lay-out and beautiful cover design. My thanks go to Sankar Narayan Mallik, who has rendered invaluable help and his expertise in reading the manuscript thoroughly and providing indispensable editorial insights. I thank him for his co-operation in my literary journey.

My love and gratitude to my family for supporting me in all my endeavours. My husband, Lalit and daughter Ishani, share my interest in travel and literature. Had it not been for them, my literary pursuits would have been difficult. We have travelled together to these far-flung destinations, and they have rendered invaluable help to me in the process of my research. Special thanks to my mother, Pratibha Ray, who is in the truest sense, a friend, philosopher and guide, and has always been a constructive critic. As a writer herself, my discussions with her during my research and writings were very helpful to me.

Thanks to all those who have extended their co-operation in my explorations: student members of the Heritage Club, IITTM Bhubaneswar, members of Rediscover Lost Heritage, the Intach family and local community members of all sites.

I express my heartfelt gratitude to my readers for their unwavering support and enthusiasm for my books. It is with immense joy and appreciation that I acknowledge the fact that your loyal readership has given my books the status of being bestsellers. Your reviews and discussions about my books have provided me with invaluable feedback and inspiration. Your enthusiasm and encouragement have fueled my creativity and propelled me to keep striving for excellence in every piece of writing I produce.

This book is a collection of experiences of my visits and travels to different temples and temple towns over time in Odisha. My research around cultural and heritage tourism intensified the interest for visiting and understanding spiritual spaces. Most of the photographs are mine and some belong to my dear students. Few have been chosen from the internet.

Through meticulous research and passionate advocacy, this book illuminates the forgotten narratives of ancient temples and cultural treasures that have shaped the identity of Odisha. As we turn the pages, we are not simply uncovering the past; we are rekindling a dialogue about the vital importance of preserving our heritage for future generations. The narratives contained within these chapters serve not only as historical artifacts but also as a compelling call to action for all of us to actively participate in the stewardship of our cultural legacy.

Dr. Adyasha Das

Gangeswari Temple

The Gangeswari Temple, located at Baiyalisbati in the Puri district of Odisha, is a significant yet lesser-known shrine dedicated to the goddess Gangeswari, a form of Shakti. This temple is an important site in the Shakta tradition, deeply intertwined with local myths and iconography that highlight the role of the divine feminine in the region's religious life. Odisha, with its rich spiritual heritage, is home to numerous temples dedicated to various forms of the goddess. While the Jagannath Temple in Puri dominates the religious consciousness of the state, many smaller shrines like the Gangeswari Temple in Baiyalisbati maintain deep local significance. Gangeswari, the presiding deity of this temple, is revered as a manifestation of Shakti, and her cult blends Vedic, Tantric, and folk elements. The temple's iconography, rituals, and the myths associated with the goddess offer insights into the complex interplay between local religious practices and broader Hindu traditions.

Baiyalisbati, a small village in the Puri district, lies about 40 kilometers from the famous Jagannath Temple. Though the exact date of the Gangeswari Temple's construction is uncertain, local oral traditions suggest it may have been built during the medieval period, under the influence of the Shakta tradition, which flourished in

Odisha from the 8th century onward. Gangeswari, being associated with both the Ganga River and the fierce aspect of the goddess, holds a prominent place in local mythology, representing both the nurturing and destructive powers of nature.

Visiting the Gangeswari temple, a model temple for the Sun temple Konark, was a long-cherished dream. Situated in Bayalisbati, the temple of Goddess Gangeswari, the Ishtadevi of kings of Ganga dynasty stands regal & dignified in its relative isolation. Gangeswari temple has a unique entrance gate and exquisite sculptures like Konark. A beautiful image of Goddess Varahi as a parshvadevi, image of Lord Indra on his Airavat elephant, captivating stone carvings depicting stories make this temple special. Images of Naga-purusha and Naga-kanya are also there.

The temple is relatively simple in structure, typical of many rural Odishan temples. It features a small yet ornate vimana (temple tower) and a jagamohana (assembly hall), constructed in the Kalinga architectural style, which is characteristic of the region. While the temple itself may not

boast the grandeur of larger Shakta shrines like the Tara Tarini Temple or the Maa Mangala Temple, it is nonetheless significant for the deeply rooted local worship and the vivid iconography of Gangeswari that it houses. The temple has an image of Muchalinda Buddha suggestive of connections with Buddhism. The exterior is decorated with Dikpalas, Dikpalikas, different forms of Shiva, Durga, Nayikas, gajasnara vidala, Chaitya medallion, hunting scene, animals and social scenes.

The deity worshipped in the sanctum of this temple is Goddess Gangeswari, the Ishta Devi (family deity) of the rulers of the Ganga dynasty. It is evident that this was a seat of tantric practices; the idols of Maa Gangeswari and the four-armed Varahi as Parsvadevi, one of the celebrated "Saptmatrikas" tongue sticking out, with a bowl of blood, a dagger, and shield amply signifies it. Apart from these, there are other images connected to tantra worship, like Chamunda. The Ganpati image adorns the ratha on the outer wall of the garbha-griha. He holds modakas in one hand, and the broken tusk in the other for writing the scriptures. This ancient temple holds immense significance within the Shaiva-Shakta tradition, where Tantra practices are central to the rituals. Goddess Gangeswari is believed to be an incarnation of Goddess Parvati. Like many Shakta temples in Odisha, Gangeswari Temple is steeped in Tantric worship, emphasizing the spiritual union of Shiva and Shakti, which is a fundamental aspect of Tantra.

Tantra Worship at Gangeswari Temple

Tantra is a spiritual path that emphasizes the worship of Shakti, the divine feminine force, in union with Shiva. The Gangeswari Temple, as a seat of Tantra, focuses on the intricate rituals that invoke this divine energy for spiritual awakening and liberation. The worship practices at this temple include:

Yantra Worship: At the Gangeswari Temple, the use of mystical diagrams known as Yantras is integral to worship. These geometric patterns are believed to represent the universe and the divine energy of the goddess. The Sri Yantra, a sacred symbol in Tantra, is frequently used during rituals to invoke the power of Gangeswari.

Mantra Chanting: The recitation of mantras, especially the goddess's bija (seed) mantras, plays a vital role in the spiritual practices at the temple. These mantras are considered highly powerful and are chanted during special Tantric rituals.

Sacrificial Offerings: The temple is known for its association with the ancient practice of Bali (sacrificial offerings), a ritual deeply rooted in Tantra. While the practice of animal sacrifice has diminished and almost disappeared over time, symbolic offerings such as coconuts, fruits, and rice are made to appease the goddess.

Auspicious Occasions and Rituals: During festivals like Durga Puja, Navaratri, and Kali Puja, the temple becomes a hub for Tantric worship. Special rituals are aimed at invoking the goddess's divine energy. During these festivals, devotees participate in rituals involving fire sacrifices (homa), offering ghee, flowers, and sacred herbs to the sacred fire to purify themselves and seek the blessings of the goddess.

Historically, the Gangeswari Temple has been a centre of spiritual learning and Tantric practice in the region. It is believed that several Tantric practitioners, or Sadhakas, from different parts of India would visit this temple for spiritual practices. The temple's secluded location made it an ideal site for the intense and often secretive practices of Tantra, which involve the mastery of the mind, body, and soul through rituals, meditation, and devotion. The surrounding area of Baiyalisbati, in the Gop block of Puri district, has a strong historical connection to ancient temples and Tantric centres. The presence of the Gangeswari Temple further underscores the deep-rooted traditions of Shaiva-Shakta worship in the region.

Imagery and Symbolism in Tantric Worship

Goddess Gangeswari's depiction at the temple carries deep symbolic meaning in the context of Tantra. She is often shown with multiple arms, holding various weapons like the trident (Trishula) and a skull cup, symbolizing her powers of destruction and regeneration. The iconography of Gangeswari echoes the concept of Kali, another form of Shakti, who represents time, death, and transformation in the Tantric tradition. The temple's imagery, from the intricate carvings on the walls to the representations of fierce goddesses, mirrors the metaphysical teachings of Tantra—where life and death, creation and destruction, are seen as complementary forces.

The temple is located amidst a picturesque village with a mighty legend kept alive by the Bayalis Bati inhabitants that links it with the Sun Temple at Konark. It

is popularly believed that Konark's chief architect, Sibei Samantaray lived at Baiyalis Bati and with his team of 1200 craftsmen, artisans, engineers and supervisors developed blueprints and finalized plans for constructing the sun temple. The masonry for Konark was transported by rafts on the Patharabhasa River close to the village.

But what is most alluring about the legend is the belief that Gangeswari Temple was a precursor to the Sun Temple, a prototype that was the miniature blueprint of the original temple. This beautifully carved temple was associated with the Ganga Vamsa kings, including Chod Ganga Dev and Narusingh Dev. The temple's architectural style bears an uncanny resemblance to the majestic Sun Temple, a UNESCO World Heritage Site. Both temples have striking similarities in the sculptures, design and iconography. No wonder it is often referred to as "Mini Konark". Patches of water bodies found are the remains of an ancient river (tributary) called Patharabhasa Nai which joined Chandrabhaga River near the main construction site of Konark temple and was a medium of transporting stones and sculptures to the construction site of the temple.

Religious heritage often transmits age-old values linked to the identity of a destination. Temples, churches, synagogues, mosques, and other religious institutions are expressions of faith inter-linking a complex range of symbolic, psychological and ideological values, including power and authority, tradition and modernity, emotion and devotion, ethic and aesthetic, theology and liturgy, individual and group, divine and human, etc.

During my recent visit to the Gangeswari temple, I found few locals playing cards and enjoying the cool evening breeze in the temple premises. Some were sprawled out on a mat and the others were lost in their strategies to

win the game, completely oblivious to the sacred power that was manifested in the temple. Are sacred spaces still considered sacred? Can people today experience this same awe in the presence of a place deemed by tradition to be holy or sacred? Or is adaptive reuse of sacred space an attempt at redefining it? Sacred spaces are now important socio-cultural public spaces for society. It is a space where people feel safe and a sense of belonging to a community that has a common belief and value system is strengthened.

References:
- Mohapatra, R. P. Temples of Orissa. Bhubaneswar: Government of Odisha, 1993.
- Dash, D. P. Tantric Cult and Temples of Odisha. New Delhi: Aryan Books, 2005.
- Marglin, F. A. Wives of the God-King: The Rituals of Devotion in India. Oxford: Oxford University Press, 1985.
- Pattnaik, D. N. Goddesses of Odisha: Tradition and Worship. Bhubaneswar: Odia Sahitya Samaj, 2010.

Pataleswara Temple

One of the ancient temples of Odisha is the Pataleswara temple, Paikapada at Therubali, Rayagada. Paikapada is famous for the Pataleshwar Shiva temple, which dates to the 9th century. It is believed that there are 99,99,999 Shiva lingams in and around the shrine. Lord Jagannath, Maa Dakhineswari Kalika, and Chamunda are the most significant deities worshiped here. People from far and near visit the shrine during the festivals of Shivaratri and Rath Yatra. A rock inscription in Brahmi script found at the Pataleswar temple commemorates the Eastern Ganga dynasty and the Suryavansha dynasty kings in Rayagada.

Declared as a tourist spot in 1992, the temple attracts thousands of devotees from across the state during the auspicious Odia month of Kartika and Shivaratri. The recent reports of valuable idols, including those of Kankali, Jai Durga, Shiva-Parvati, Laxmi Paduka, and Shiva Linga, being smuggled from a heritage site underscore the urgent need for conservation measures. This temple, constructed during the reign of Jeypore King Ramakrishna Dev in 766 AD, is not only an architectural marvel but also a significant cultural artifact engraved with Devanagari script on its pillars. Such historical sites are vital to our understanding of heritage and identity, serving as tangible links to our past.

According to temple priest Kali Prasad Mishra, the shrine is traditionally believed to have been established by Lord Balaram during the Dwapara Yuga. This narrative enriches the temple's significance, intertwining mythology with history. Lord Balaram's discovery of the Shiva linga within a cave and subsequent construction of the temple illustrates how these sites are often steeped in local lore and spiritual importance.

Significance of Ancient Temples

Ancient temples like this one are not merely places of worship; they represent a confluence of art, culture, and community. They serve as centres for spiritual practice and social gatherings, reflecting the values and beliefs of the societies that built them. The architectural styles found in these temples often showcase intricate craftsmanship and regional influences, contributing to a rich legacy of cultural heritage across India.

In comparision, other temples named Pataleswar across India also embody similar historical and architectural significance. For instance, the Pataleshwar Cave Temple in Pune dates to the 8th century and is carved out of rock, exemplifying the unique rock-cut architecture prevalent in ancient Indian temples. Like the temple in Jeypore, Pataleswar serves as a testament to the artistic ingenuity and religious devotion of its time.

The preservation of such sites is crucial for maintaining our cultural legacy. Temples are not just relics; they are living monuments that continue to inspire devotion and attract visitors from around the world. Their architectural grandeur often draws comparisons with globally recognized sites like the Konark Sun Temple or Khajuraho temples, both celebrated for their intricate designs and historical significance. In Odisha, for example, ancient temples are integral to local culture and tourism, providing economic benefits while fostering a sense of identity among residents. The loss of artifacts from temples like the one in Jeypore diminishes not only their historical value but also their role as communal spaces where traditions are upheld.

In conclusion, ancient temples serve as vital repositories of our cultural heritage. They encapsulate historical narratives that enrich our understanding of identity and community. As we face challenges such as artifact smuggling and neglect, it becomes imperative to implement robust conservation measures to safeguard these architectural marvels for future generations.

Barahi Temple

The Prachi Valley is home to several significant Shakta temples:
1. Varahi Temple at Chaurasi: A temple dedicated to Goddess Varahi, showcasing unique architectural styles.
2. Ambika Temple at Kenduli Deuli (Kenduli): Devoted to Goddess Ambika, this temple holds historical and cultural importance.
3. Durga Temple at Nua-Satanga (Motia): A temple honouring Goddess Durga, known for its local reverence.
4. Durga Temple at Kudapatna (Amanakuda): Another sacred site dedicated to Goddess Durga, reflecting ancient traditions.
5. Durga Temple at Adaspur: Famous for its spiritual significance, this temple is also dedicated to Durga.
6. Rama-Chandi Temple at Narisho: A temple for Goddess Rama-Chandi, blending local folklore and religious practices.
7. Hara-Chandi Temple at Bisimatri: A temple dedicated to Goddess Hara-Chandi, associated with local worship rituals.
8. Kakatei Temple at Kakatpur: Known for its connection with Goddess Kakatei, this site attracts many devotees.

9. Mangala Temple at Kakatpur: A highly revered temple dedicated to Goddess Mangala, with deep-rooted traditions.
10. Dakshina Chandi Temple at Mangalapur: A temple devoted to Goddess Dakshina Chandi, recognized for its religious significance.
11. Charchika Temple at Narasinghpurhat: A temple for Goddess Charchika, known for its unique iconography.
12. Chandaghanta Chamunda Temple at Nuagaon: Dedicated to Goddess Chandaghanta Chamunda, it holds significant spiritual value.
13. Durga Temple at Ambapara: A sacred site for worshipping Durga, part of the local temple landscape.
14. Chitresvari Temple at Chitresvari: Known for its devotion to Goddess Chitresvari, this temple is culturally important.
15. Durga Temple at Narisho: Another temple dedicated to Durga, reflecting the area's strong Shakta traditions.
16. Adya Kali Temple at Govindarampatna: A temple devoted to Adya Kali, showcasing the area's dedication to Shakta worship.

These temples highlight the rich Shakta traditions and spiritual heritage of the Prachi Valley.

A long-cherished dream come true event was my visit to the Barahi Temple at Chaurasi, a famous Shakta shrine of the Prachi Valley of Odisha. I am glad that I chose a scorching May afternoon as I had the temple all to myself. It was blazing hot, but a gentle breeze started blowing soon after I arrived and the coconut trees all around created a magical web of light and shade. Famous as the beauty of the Prachi Valley, careful restoration work has been

done here. The ancient, 9th century temple is dedicated to Goddess Barahi, the female counterpart of Varaha, the boar incarnation of Vishnu. One among the Sapta-matrika group of Vaishnavi, Maheswari, Brahmani, Indrani, Kaumari and Chamunda, this is a rare temple dedicated to Barahi alone. Barahi is an incarnation of Bhu Devi.

Varahi is worshipped by three practices of Hinduism: Shaivism (devotees of Shiva), Vaishnavism (devotees of Vishnu), and especially Shaktism (goddess worship). She is usually worshipped at night, using secretive Vamamarga Tantric practices. The Buddhist goddesses Vajravārāhī and Marichi have their origins from the Hindu goddess Varahi.

There are intricate carvings all over the temple walls, with number of erotic panels suggesting tantric rites. The Barahi temple of Chaurasi is decorated with both cult images as well as non-iconic figures. The central niches of the *bada* houses the *parshvadevata* images of Ganesha and Surya. The images of Surya and Ganesha are the *parshvadevatas* of western (back) and southern sides of the *bada* respectively.

I spent the entire afternoon by myself till a group of young boys came to shoot their reels. They said they liked the isolated temple and often used it as a backdrop to their songs. The door to the inner chamber was locked and as

I strained through the barred door to have a glimpse of the Goddess, the gardener of the property got a key and allowed me to enter the sanctum sanctorum. The life-size image of Barahi was so captivating! Seated in *lalitasana* on a pedestal, the image bears the face of a boar and body of a divine woman. Her right hand holds a fish while with the left, she holds a *kapala*. Barahi is represented with a third eye on her forehead and hair decorated in the form of spiral coils. The beauty of this image lies in her big belly to indicate her as holding the universe in her womb. On the slab behind, two *vidyadharas* are represented each on either side.

Barahi, one of the Mother Goddesses, a manifestation of 64 Yoginis and the counterpart of Varaha-Vishnu was created to annihilate powerful demons like Chanda, Munda, Sumbha, Nisumbha, Raktavirjya and the Tripura Vijayi Mahisasura. The goddess Varahi associated with the other mothers-Brahmani, Maheswari, Koumari, Vaisnavi, Indrani and Chamunda assisted Ambika in her combat against the demons.

A life-size image of Barahi (6 ft. 1 in. high and 2 ft. 9 in. wide) is enshrined in the temple at Chaurasi in Prachi

valley in perfect state of preservation. Seated in *lalitasana* on a cushion placed on a plain legged seat with her hanging right leg resting on a life-like buffalo, the figure holds in her right hand a fish and in the left a blood-cup. Adorned with finger rings, anklets, *valayas*, armlets, necklace, large ear studs and a tiara over the hair which rises upwards in spiral coils, the three-eyed deity is pot-bellied and is clad in a dhoti. The plain halo is oval, the back of the figure is cut out of the oblong back-slab. The temple enshrining the image of Barahi comes in the order of Khakhara and bears resemblance to the Gouri temple at Bhubaneswar. On stylistic grounds the temple and the image are assignable to the early part of 10th century A.D. In the Jagamohana of the temple are two loose sculptures of Barahi seated in *Maharajalilasana*, having a skull cup and a fish in two hands. The other is four-armed holding in the lower left a skull cup, in the upper left a rosary, a water-pot in the lower right (upper left broken) associated with the mount buffalo and kneeling devotee. These two images were probably enshrined in some other temples in the locality. Barahi is believed to be the Shakti of Varaha. In the Tantric text 'Varahi Tantra' mention has been made of five forms of Varahi i.e., Svapna Varahi, Canda Varahi, Mahi Varahi (Bhairavi), Krcca Varahi and Matsya Varahi. The description of Matsya Varahi closely corresponds to the image enshrined in the temple. Apart from the erotic sculptures all over the temple walls, there are several decorative motifs-attractive *Salabhanjikas* and *bajramastakas*, battle scenes of Ramayana and the imposing Naga *stambhas*.

The Barahi Temple of Chaurasi is a remarkable example of ancient Odishan temple architecture, showcasing intricate details in both structure and sculpture. The *vimana* of the temple, rising about 27 feet, belongs to the *pancaratha*

khakhara order of architecture, a style distinguished by its unique wagon vault-shaped superstructure. The temple's *vimana* bears resemblance to the Gauri temple of Bhubaneswar and stands on a rectangular base, supported by a plain *pishta*. The *gandi* or upper tower of the *vimana* is divided into two storeys, further embellished with erotic sculptures and *khakhara mundi* motifs. This combination of structural complexity and decorative features can be compared to other temples of the period, particularly the Gauri temple. The *bisama* portion, located above the *gandi*, features perforated *jali* work and a central motif, including a *caitya* window medallion flanked by dwarf figures. The temple's *mastaka* or head is crowned by a *kalasa*, a symbol of auspiciousness.

The *jagamohana* or assembly hall is rectangular, measuring about 31 by 23 feet, and follows the *pidha deula* architectural style. It has an 18-foot height, and the *bada* is divided into *pabhaga*, *jangha*, and *baranda*. The central projections of the northern and southern walls contain latticed windows with criss-cross designs and are adorned with intricate carvings, including nagini figures, scroll work, and lotus motifs. The roof of the *jagamohana* has two terraces, ornamented with scenes from the Ramayana, hunting scenes, and animal processions. Sculpturally, the Barahi Temple stands out for its detailed depictions of both cult images and non-iconic figures. The *parshvadevata* figures include Surya on the western side and Ganesha on the southern side. The image of Surya, depicted seated on his chariot pulled by seven horses, is particularly striking with its intricate detailing. Ganesha is represented holding a variety of attributes such as a hatchet, a pot of sweets, a broken tusk, and a rosary, symbolizing different aspects of his persona.

The presiding deity of the temple, Goddess Barahi, is enshrined in the sanctum. The image of Varahi is noted for its tantric associations, reflecting the Kaula cult traditions of the region. The temple's connection with tantric worship, particularly evident in the erotic sculptures and the portrayal of *kapalika* participants, underscores its significance within the broader spectrum of Shakti worship in medieval India.

Madhav Temple

Our visit to Niali was certainly not impromptu. It was a drive I had undertaken thousand times in my mind. Niali was my father's first posting as an engineer in the State Government's PWD department. Yet strangely we had never gone back there. I had travelled on that road visiting the series of Prachi Valley temples in my bucket list. Like many thriving civilizations of the past - the Aryan, Egyptian, Babylonian, Assyrian which were founded and rose to prominence on the banks of rivers, Prachi Valley Civilization, a glorious civilization of Odisha, flourished on the banks of River Prachi. There are many holy rivers in the land of India- Ganga, Godavari, Brahmaputra, Cauvery, Shipra, Prachi etc. As stated in the Padma Purana, Prachi is believed to have originated from the feet of Brahma. The worship of Madhava, one of the twenty-four manifestations of Lord Vishnu in Prachi Valley, had immense influence in that area. There are twelve ancient Madhava temples found in the Prachi valley: Adaspur Madhav, Kendubil Madhab, Gupta Madhav, Janjali Madhav Lataharan Madhav, Lalit Madhav, Kalara Madhav, Nibharan Madhav, Jatayu Madhav. Raghunathpur Madhav, Neela Madhav and Durga Madhav.

The Prachi Valley, located in the eastern part of Odisha, India, is an ancient cultural landscape with significant historical, religious, and archaeological importance. The valley, which stretches around 60 kms in length, is traversed by the Prachi River, a tributary of the Mahanadi River. This region has been a cradle of cultural and religious practices from the early historic period, and the numerous temples that dot the valley are testimony to its religious importance. Among these, the Madhav Temple stands out as an iconic structure with unique historical and architectural attributes.

The Madhav Temple: Historical Background

The Madhav Temple, situated at Madhav village in the Prachi Valley, is a significant example of early medieval temple architecture in Odisha. Dating back to the 9th-11th century CE, the temple represents the flourishing Somavamsi dynasty, which played a critical role in the development of Odisha's temple architecture. Although the exact dates of construction are still debated among scholars, the temple is typically attributed to the later part of the Somavamsi period, before the rise of the Eastern Ganga dynasty. Odisha during the early medieval period witnessed a synthesis of religious traditions, with Shaivism, Vaishnavism, Shaktism, and Buddhism all coexisting and influencing temple art and architecture.

The Madhav Temple, dedicated to Lord Vishnu (Madhava), is an important Vaishnavite temple in this religiously diverse landscape. It represents a link between the broader *Pancharatra* tradition of Vaishnavism and local Odisha cultic practices.

The Temple is built in the *pancharatha* design. The Vimana is of Rekha Deula, Jagamohana is of Pidha deula and the Natamandapa is flat-roofed and renovated by Archaeological Survey of India. The motifs depicting serpents, *naayikas*, devatas etc are intricate. Dating back to the 13th century it was built by the Eastern Ganga dynasty. Rare images of Dasa-Avatar of Vishnu, a big Sudarshan Chakra made up of Black granite stone, Ananta Sayana of Vishnu on the walls of Jagamohana and Natamandapa etc are found here. The outer walls of the temple are carved with beautiful Pauranic images from Krishna Lila & Mahabharata. Some erotic carvings can also be found on the outer wall of the temple.

Prachi is considered as the mainstream of the River Mahanadi which became dry when it changed its course. But the coastline of the river is dotted with wonderful monuments, attractive rural vistas, folk arts, music and handicrafts, cuisine, ancient ports etc. In the

Prachi Mahatmya, edited and compiled by Sri Balaram Dash, there are references to Dvadasa Madhava of Prachi Valley.

The central icon of the Madhab temple, Madhaba is a rare image. The upper left arm holds Gada, lower left Sudarshana Chakra, upper right a full-blown lotus and lower right, Shankha. In the Jagamohana a rare image of Durga is found. She is worshipped as the sister of Madhaba. Many festivals like Janmashtami, Ekadashi and special festivals in Maagha and Vaishakha months are celebrated here. The main attraction is the very old idol of Garuda, which is made of black sandstone, apart from various rare statues.

There is lot of speculation regarding deterioration of temples of the Prachi Valley. The temples and monuments constructed with bricks and mortar met their natural decay in course of time. Water, in either liquid or vapour form accelerates the process of deterioration. Stone, bricks and metals deteriorate faster in the presence of water while decay is slow under dry conditions. Another factor of deterioration is climate and the proximity to sea. Mughal invasion is also the reason for the transfer of many statues to smaller, lesser-known temples to keep them hidden.

The fast pace of development and emergence of newer trends has led to drastic changes in tourist behaviour, especially with reference to temple visits. With villages becoming modernized and locals travelling out for jobs, the old-world power of temples on devotees has been redefined. It is more a niche segment of people who visit temples these days. The motivational factors for doing so could be Learning, Self-growth, Harmonising with Nature, and Spirituality. Motivations to visit temples have significant impacts on life satisfaction among Millennial tourists and devotees. I spoke to several village devotees who were gathered around the temple and nearby shops. A quaint teashop in front of the temple was our preferred point. I was lucky to meet Haramani Pushpalak, a spiry woman of eighty who ran around the temple like a 16-year-old! She spoke about the profile of people visiting the temple and animatedly discussed the major fairs and festivals.

Religious Significance

The Madhav Temple's dedication to Vishnu is significant in the context of the Vaishnavite revival in Odisha, which occurred during the early medieval period. This period saw a surge in the construction of temples dedicated to Vishnu, in part due to the influence of Pancharatra and Bhagavata traditions of Vaishnavism. These traditions emphasized the worship of Vishnu in his various forms and incarnations, including Krishna and Narayana.

The Prachi Valley was a prominent centre for syncretic religious practices, where Hinduism, Buddhism, and Jainism coexisted, and often influenced each other. The Madhav Temple, with its focus on Vaishnavism, reflects this religious dynamism, as Vishnu worship integrated elements of older local and regional deities. The Madhava form of Vishnu worship at this temple is linked to regional folklore and mythological narratives that further establish its cultural importance in the Prachi Valley. The presence of other temples, including Shiva and Shakti temples, in the vicinity indicates a complex religious landscape where multiple traditions thrived together.

Preservation and Archaeological Importance

The Prachi Valley, including the Madhav Temple, is of

immense archaeological value, not just for understanding the religious life of early medieval Odisha but also for studying the development of temple architecture in the region. The temple is under the protection of

the Archaeological Survey of India (ASI), which has undertaken efforts to preserve the remaining structure. Scholarly research on the Madhav Temple, as well as on other temples in the valley, has highlighted the need for more extensive conservation work. Epigraphical evidence from inscriptions found in the vicinity of the temple has shed light on the socio-political context of its construction, including the patronage provided by local rulers and the priestly class. Archaeologists have also suggested that the Prachi Valley, with its ancient waterways and agricultural fertility, was a hub of commerce and cultural exchange, further amplifying the importance of temples like Madhav in the region's history.

The Madhav Temple in Prachi Valley is a key monument in the study of Odisha's temple architecture and religious history. Its architectural features are emblematic of the Kalinga style, while its religious significance highlights the importance of Vaishnavism during the early medieval period in Odisha. As a part of the larger archaeological and cultural landscape of the Prachi Valley, the Madhav Temple stands as a symbol of Odisha's rich heritage, connecting the region's past with its religious and artistic legacy. Further research and preservation efforts are crucial to understanding the full historical context of this temple and the Prachi Valley at large. In recent years, scholars have called for more interdisciplinary studies combining archaeology, epigraphy, and religious studies to fully unravel the significance of the Madhav Temple and its surroundings.

References:
- Nanda, Ramakrishna, Compiler - Viswa Parichaya (O)- P/341 2. Ray, P.K. Editor-Archaeological Survey

Report, 1974-75- P/1 3. Senapati, Nilamani, editor- Orissa District Gazetteers (Puri), P/14
- R. Balasubramaniam, Kalinga Temples of Orissa: Architecture, Art, and Cultural Heritage. Delhi: Pratibha Prakashan, 2015.
- B. K. Mohapatra, "The Temple Architecture of Odisha: A Study in Historical Continuity," Indian Historical Review, Vol. 42, No. 1, 2015.
- A. Singh, "The Syncretic Traditions of the Prachi Valley: Archaeological Evidence and Religious Narratives," South Asian Studies Journal, 2021.
- S. Patnaik, Odisha's Sacred Landscape: The Prachi Valley Temples. Bhubaneswar: Odisha State Museum, 2018.

Sobhaneswar Temple

The ancient 12th Century Sobhaneswar temple was built with the royal patronage of King Anangabhima Deva II, the illustrious king of the Ganga dynasty. Massive in size yet delicate in the exquisite sculptures, the temple is a protected monument site of the State Archaeology Department. Situated in Niali, the temple is in the middle of a small, nondescript village. A valued inscription on the wall of the Jagamohana mentions about Vaidyanath, a Nagavamsi king, who possibly took up the repair and maintenance of the temple after the Ganga rule. Bagu Nana, the priest of the temple showed how the inscription was a mixture of several languages. I could spot Sanskrit and Hindi words but put together it was not easy to read.

The Sobhaneswar Temple, located in Niali within the Prachi Valley of Odisha, is an ancient and architecturally significant Shiva temple that dates back to the early medieval period. The Prachi Valley itself is a region of immense historical and cultural importance, home to a plethora of temples, monasteries, and religious sites that trace the evolution of religious and cultural practices in Odisha. The Sobhaneswar Temple, dedicated to Lord Shiva, is one of the notable monuments in this valley and reflects the rich temple-building tradition of Odisha, particularly during the Somavamsi and Ganga dynasties.

The Temple is believed to have been built during the 11th-12th century CE, a period that witnessed the flourishing of temple architecture under the patronage of the Somavamsi kings and later the Eastern Ganga rulers. The temple's construction corresponds to the later part of the Somavamsi rule, which was marked by a growing emphasis on temple building and the consolidation of Shaivism as a dominant religious tradition in Odisha. While the exact date of the temple's construction is still debated, epigraphic evidence suggests that it was an important religious centre during the medieval period, attracting devotees from the surrounding regions. The temple is part of the wider religious landscape of the Prachi Valley, which was known for its religious syncretism, with Shaivism, Vaishnavism, Shaktism, and Buddhism all thriving in the area.

The presiding deity of the temple is Harihara, a fusion of Vishnu (Hari) and Shiva (Hara). Many of the sculptures have lost their finesse to erosion caused by wind and water logging. The renovation work is on which may take few years due to the slow chemical process. As per details of the temple documented by the Indira Gandhi National Centre for the Arts, certain portions have been renovated successfully such as the lower roof of the temple. The temple celebrates several fairs and festivals and according to the locals I interacted with, devotees from nearby spots continue to visit this revered temple.

The temporary museum within the premises of the temple is a shed displaying rare sculptures found in and around the site. Some Vishnu idols (Madhava) had been shifted from the nearby Madhava temple to Sobhaneswar to prevent the idols from being demolished by Moghul attackers. Eight magnificent images of Madhava and one image of Varaha are kept inside the temple compound. A

huge Nandi has recently been made at the entrance of the main gate which adorns the exterior of the temple. A rare statue of Buddha, in Dhyana Mudra is one of the main attractions of the temple.

Sculptures of Dikpalaks and Dikpalikas, guardians of directions are engraved on the side walls of the temple. These Guardians of Direction are deities who rule the different directions of space according to Hinduism and Vajrayāna Buddhism, especially Kālachakra. Ganesha and Karthikeya are prominent as devatas. A striking image of Lakulisha is found on the side walls. Lakulisha was a prominent Shaivite revivalist, reformist and preceptor of the doctrine of the Pashupatas, one of the oldest sects of Shaivism. Some scholars revere Lakulisha as the founder of the Pashupata sect.

The Sobhaneswar Temple is an excellent example of the Kalinga style of temple architecture, which is known for its distinct structural and decorative features. The temple exhibits the Rekha Deula form, a characteristic type of temple architecture seen in Odisha, where the sanctum (garbhagriha) is surmounted by a curvilinear tower.

The architectural components of the Sobhaneswar Temple are divided into two key sections:

Vimana (Sanctum): The vimana is the main structure housing the deity and is surmounted by a towering curvilinear shikhara (spire). The spire rises in a vertical manner with a series of horizontal mouldings, tapering towards the top. The Sobhaneswar Temple's vimana follows the typical Rekha Deula design, which is noted for its vertical emphasis and compact form.

Jagamohana (Mandapa): The temple also features a Pidha Deula style jagamohana, or assembly hall, where worshippers gather. The roof of the jagamohana is tiered and pyramidal in structure, built using horizontal layers that gradually recede in size as they rise.

The temple is built using sandstone, a common material for temple construction in Odisha, and the exterior walls are richly ornamented with carvings. The sculptur-

al work on the Sobhaneswar Temple includes depictions of mythological figures, floral motifs, and scenes from Shaivite iconography. Particularly noteworthy are the intricately carved figures of deities, celestial beings, and apsaras (heavenly maidens), as well as representations of ganas (attendants of Shiva), which are consistent with the Shaivite theme of the temple.

The temple's iconography is focused on Lord Shiva, with several sculptures of the deity in his various forms. The Shivalinga in the sanctum is worshipped as Sobhaneswar Mahadeva, a manifestation of Shiva associated with the local folklore and religious traditions of the Prachi Valley.

The Sobhaneswar Temple holds significant religious importance as a centre of Shaivism in the Prachi Valley. The dedication of the temple to Shiva highlights the dominant role that Shaivism played in the religious life of the region during the early medieval period. Shaivism in Odisha, especially during the reign of the Somavamsi and Ganga dynasties, was marked by the construction of large and small temples dedicated to various forms of Shiva, such as Lingaraja in Bhubaneswar and Sobhaneswar in Niali. The temple's location in the Prachi Valley is also significant due to the valley's long-standing association with religious syncretism. The Prachi River itself is often regarded as a sacred entity, and several rituals and religious festivals are conducted along its banks, drawing devotees to the temple during auspicious occasions. The Sobhaneswar Temple, with its Shaivite focus, has been central to the Mahashivaratri celebrations, attracting pilgrims from nearby regions.

The temple also reflects the regional religious traditions of the Prachi Valley, where local deities and folk religious practices were integrated into mainstream Hinduism. Sobhaneswar, as a local manifestation of Shiva, is linked with the agricultural and riverine culture of the area, and the temple played an important role in the life of the local agrarian communities.

The Sobhaneswar Temple is an important archaeological site and is currently protected under the supervision of the Archaeological Survey of India (ASI). Due to the temple's age and exposure to the elements, it has undergone significant wear and tear, and conservation efforts have been initiated to preserve its architectural and artistic features. Despite some deterioration, much of the original structure remains intact, providing valuable insights into early medieval temple architecture in Odisha.

The temple's epigraphic records are also of archaeological interest. Inscriptions found at the site provide information about the temple's patrons, including references to local kings and noble families who supported its construction and maintenance. These inscriptions also shed light on the religious and social life of the region, offering clues about the local religious practices and the significance of Shiva worship in the Prachi Valley. Scholarly research on the Sobhaneswar Temple has emphasized its importance in the broader context of Odishan temple architecture. The temple's Rekha Deula form, intricate carvings, and iconographic program are reflective of the artistic developments during the Somavamsi and Ganga periods, particularly in how they integrated regional and pan-Indian religious elements.

The Sobhaneswar Temple at Niali stands as a testament to the rich cultural and religious history of the Prachi Valley and Odisha's medieval period. Architecturally, the temple is a significant example of the Kalinga style of temple construction, with its well-preserved Rekha Deula and Pidha Deula structures. Religiously, the temple is an important centre of Shaivism, reflecting the dominant religious trends of the early medieval period and the syncretic religious practices that characterized the Prachi Valley. Despite the challenges posed by time and weathering, the Sobhaneswar Temple continues to be a site of worship and an important part of Odisha's heritage. Ongoing archaeological research and conservation efforts are crucial in preserving this valuable monument and furthering our understanding of the region's history and cultural development.

References
- S. Mishra, Temples of Odisha: A Historical and Cultural Study, Bhubaneswar: Orissa State Museum, 2016.
- M. Pattnaik, "Shaivism in Early Medieval Odisha: A Study of Iconography and Architecture," Journal of Indian History and Culture, Vol. 28, 2019.
- R. Patra, "The Archaeology of the Prachi Valley: Uncovering Religious Syncretism in Odisha," Indian Archaeological Review, Vol. 15, 2021.
- K. Rout, Odisha's Sacred Temples: From Early Historic to Medieval Times, New Delhi: Pratibha Prakashan, 2020.

Swapneswar Temple

The Swapneswar Shiva Temple, located near Pipli in the Puri district of Odisha, is an ancient and lesser-known temple dedicated to Lord Shiva. Although not widely documented in scholarly records, the temple holds historical, architectural, and religious significance, contributing to the rich cultural landscape of Odisha. Odisha, known for its magnificent temples, boasts numerous lesser-known and undocumented temples that speak volumes about its past. Swapneswar Shiva Temple is a testament to this heritage, standing amidst the countryside as a forgotten gem, awaiting proper recognition and restoration.

This temple can be dated back to around 6th-7th Century. The ancient temple locally known as Swapneswar Mahadev is located beside Ghateswar temple, ahead of Pipli, Odisha. Made of square Khandlite stone blocks without any binding or cement, (as found in temples of 11th and 12th century in Odisha), it lies forgotten and anonymous. Ghateswar Nana, the priest of the Ghateswar temple invited us to the mandap as we were caught in a sudden downpour. From our vantage point atop the mandap, we could see the dense vegetation covering the temple on all sides. Later, a closer look revealed the roots that had gripped the stones and could pull it down any moment.

A picturesque village, it is dotted with temples and a

neat row of houses. The temple needs urgent and immediate attention towards its restoration and preservation. Ancient village temples are more than just architectural relics; they are vibrant symbols of cultural heritage, spiritual significance, and community identity. The resurrection and preservation of ancient village temples are vital for maintaining cultural heritage, spiritual continuity, and community identity. It requires a concerted effort from local communities, experts, and governmental bodies to protect these sacred sites for future generations.

One of the unique aspects of the Swapneswar Shiva Temple is the rustic setting in which it is located. Surrounded by farmland and trees, the temple offers a sense of serenity and historical continuity. The structure, though modest in comparison to the grander temples of Bhubaneswar or Konark, holds an important place in the region's religious practices. Like many small Shiva temples in rural Odisha, it is central to local religious life, with villagers organizing rituals during festivals such as Mahashivaratri.

However, due to the lack of formal recognition and conservation, the temple has suffered significant degradation. Parts of the structure have collapsed, and the

carvings are eroded, posing the risk of complete loss of this architectural heritage.

Anonymous Temples in Odisha: An Underexplored Heritage

Odisha is a land of temples, and while monumental structures like the Lingaraja Temple in Bhubaneswar or the Jagannath Temple in Puri are widely studied, there are hundreds of anonymous, undocumented temples scattered throughout the countryside. These temples, like the Swapneswar Shiva Temple, often go unnoticed by both scholars and the public. Built during various periods—ranging from the early medieval to the colonial era—these temples are integral to the local culture and history but remain outside the scope of mainstream heritage conservation efforts.

The reasons for their anonymity are manifold:

Geographical Isolation: Many of these temples are in rural or remote areas, far from urban centres, where they are seldom visited by researchers or tourists.

Historical Neglect: Due to a focus on larger and more famous temples, these smaller structures have often been neglected in historical and archaeological documentation.

Lack of Written Records: Many of these temples were built by local communities rather than royal patrons, which means they were often not mentioned in inscriptions or historical texts.

Cultural Transition: Over time, cultural shifts and the migration of populations have led to the abandonment or neglect of certain temples, leaving them undocumented.

These temples, while often smaller and simpler in design than their famous counterparts, are nevertheless rich in local religious practices and traditions. They are living embodiments of regional folklore, community rituals, and the architectural evolution of the region.

The first step towards preserving these forgotten temples is proper identification and documentation. This can be achieved through a combination of modern technologies and traditional methods:

Local communities are often the best source of information about undocumented temples. Engaging villagers in identifying significant but neglected religious structures is key. Oral histories, local legends, and folk narratives can offer valuable insights into the origins of these temples.

Archaeologists and historians need to conduct extensive field surveys in rural Odisha. Mapping the landscape, visiting remote areas, and cataloguing the temples—no matter how small—can create a comprehensive database of these structures.

Technologies like Geographical Information Systems (GIS) and satellite imagery can help locate temples that are off the beaten path. These tools can be especially useful in identifying ancient religious structures that have been overgrown by vegetation or obscured by rural development.

Where possible, inscriptions on the temple walls or nearby stone slabs should be examined to establish historical timelines and patronage details. These inscriptions are often in ancient Odia, Sanskrit, or Prakrit, requiring experts in epigraphy to decode their messages.

Once identified, the next crucial step is restoration and conservation. Odisha's anonymous temples face several threats, including:

Weathering: The harsh climatic conditions of the

region, especially during the monsoon, take a toll on the ancient stone structures. Over time, erosion damages the intricate carvings and structural integrity of the temples.

Vegetation Overgrowth: Many of these temples are overgrown by trees and shrubs, which can cause physical damage to the structures, as roots infiltrate the stone and weaken the foundation.

Vandalism and Neglect: The lack of formal recognition often leads to temples being vandalized or used for non-religious purposes, leading to their further deterioration.

To address these issues, the following steps can be taken:

Government and ASI Involvement: The Archaeological Survey of India (ASI), along with the State Archaeology

Department, should prioritize these anonymous temples for restoration projects. This would involve structural reinforcement, cleaning, and the preservation of original carvings.

Public Awareness and Tourism: Raising public awareness about these temples can encourage both local and international tourism, creating an incentive for their preservation. Proper signage, inclusion in heritage tourism circuits, and promotion through local festivals can bring attention to these hidden gems.

Local Artisans and Restoration Experts: Involving local artisans, who are well-versed in traditional methods of temple construction, can be invaluable in restoring these temples in a manner that remains true to their original style. Similarly, modern conservation experts can apply techniques to stabilize and preserve the temples while ensuring that future generations can enjoy their cultural richness.

The Swapneswar Shiva Temple near Pipli is emblematic of the many undocumented temples scattered across Odisha, each with its own historical and religious significance. These temples, though often neglected, are crucial in understanding the broader cultural and architectural heritage of the region. With proper identification, documentation, and restoration efforts, these temples can be saved from the brink of obscurity, ensuring that their beauty and significance endure for future generations. By combining modern technology with community involvement and traditional craftsmanship, Odisha's anonymous temples can be revived and re-integrated into the fabric of the state's cultural identity.

The Gajasimha Mandapa

Odisha, a state rich in cultural and historical heritage, is often celebrated for its grand temples as the Konark Sun Temple, the Jagannath Temple, Lingaraja Temple etc. However, beyond these monumental structures lies a forgotten world of lost heritage—abandoned temples, ancient mandapas, and mysterious sculptures scattered across the landscape, waiting to be rediscovered and revived. These structures, often hidden in plain sight, are a testament to the once-thriving architectural and cultural prowess of ancient Odisha.

One such forgotten marvel is the Gajasimha Mandapa, a massive square stone structure found in Naranagada of Khurda district. This site, relatively unknown outside local folklore, holds fascinating legends that connect it to the powerful Eastern Ganga dynasty, particularly to Langula Narasingha Deva I, the builder of the Konark Sun Temple. Alongside this, the remnants of an ancient temple and the broken sculpture of Goddess Chamunda further reflect the rich religious history of the region.

A successful heritage exploration drive led us to the Gajasimha Mandapa, a huge square sized ancient stone adorned with intricate stone art carved all over it. There are interesting legends associated with it. Locals believe it was used as the seating place of Eastern Ganga

King Langula Narasingha Deva (Narasingha Deva I), the builder of famous Konark Sun Temple. It is said that the Gajapati used to come on his royal elephant and stepped on to the Mandapa straight from atop the elephant to have discussions with his subjects. There were no steps to climb to its top. Thus, it is evident that the King used to land directly over the Mandapa from his elephant. It is difficult to ascertain the exact construction era of this magnificent stone architecture; however, if the local traditions, style of construction and archaeological remains found in and around the site are to be taken into consideration, it may be around 700 years old. Near to it, we could see the ruined remains of an ancient temple which had the broken early sculpture of Goddess Chamunda, once considered the primary deity.

The Ruins of the Chamunda Temple

Nearby the Gajasimha Mandapa lie the ruined remains of an ancient temple, once dedicated to Goddess Chamunda, a fierce form of the Mother Goddess and a representation of Shakti. The temple, now in a dilapidated state, is marked by the presence of a broken sculpture of Chamunda, which hints at the temple's past glory. Chamunda, depicted in her terrifying form with sunken eyes and skeletal features, was a deity worshipped for her protective and destructive powers. The sculpture of Chamunda, although broken, exhibits the fine craftsmanship typical of Odisha's early medieval period.

The temple's destruction could have occurred due to several factors, including natural disasters, neglect, or historical invasions that led to the abandonment of many religious structures. The presence of Chamunda's broken image signifies the fall of a once-important centre of worship, reflecting the broader story of the lost religious sites in Odisha.

The ancient Mandapa in a dilapidated state

The original temple that housed Chamunda as the primary deity is now lost and replaced by a restored version. Though broken, the features of the statue are unmistakable. Chamunda is depicted as adorned by ornaments of bones and skulls. She wears a Yajnopavita (a sacred thread worn by Hindu priests) of skulls. She wears a jata mukuta, that is, headdress formed of piled, matted hair tied with snakes or skull ornaments. The goddess has an emaciated body and shrunken belly which shows protruding ribs and veins as well as bare teeth, protruding tongue and sunken eyes.

Times have changed and the villagers are caught up in their pursuit of new jobs. The fearsome Chamunda statue lies forgotten, waiting for a rightful place in a temple and the hearts of local devotees. Chamunda is a fearsome aspect of Shakti, also known as Chamundi, Chamundeswari and

Charchika. She is one of the Saptamatrika's or seven divine Goddesses. She is also one of the chief Yoginis, a group of sixty-four Tantric goddesses. Efforts were made to spread heritage awareness among locals to protect this century old wonderful edifice.

The Gajasimha Mandapa and the ruined Chamunda temple are not isolated examples. Across Odisha, there are numerous undocumented and forgotten temples, mandapas, and other historical structures that have fallen into neglect. These sites, often found in rural or remote areas, are vital pieces of Odisha's cultural and architectural history.

The Gajasimha Mandapa, along with the ruins of the Chamunda temple, represents the vast and often overlooked cultural heritage of Odisha. These structures are silent witnesses to the region's rich history, standing as reminders of a time when Odisha's rulers, like Langula Narasingha Deva I, were patrons of great architectural and cultural endeavors. By identifying, documenting, and restoring such forgotten sites, Odisha can reclaim its lost heritage and ensure that future generations continue to learn from and appreciate its ancient past.

Amuhan Deula

Conserving heritage is important because it reflects and builds local community identities, assists in promoting sustainability and provides a sense of place. Conservation of heritage resources, provision of tourism infrastructure and local socioeconomic development are all inter-related. Strengthening local community engagement through active participation is pertinent to ensure success of heritage conservation and tourism promotion. Engaging local community in heritage conservation collaboratively with other stakeholders is crucial as it has the potential to transform values, practices and overall behaviour towards sustainability.

This belief was further strengthened after our interaction with the community members of village Sebatipur who joined hands with us in our exploration of this lost temple. Our efforts were also focused on documenting

places in their cultural and national dimensions, and in their historical and contemporary character.

Situated in Sebatipur-Paschimapari village in the Delanga Tehsil of Puri district, Amuhan Deula is an abandoned temple. Architecturally and based on local information, this temple can be assigned to a construction period close to 17th century A.D. i.e. the Bhoi Dynasty's ruling period over Odisha. The presiding deity of this temple is absent and there is no documentation of any kind available. There is, however, a possibility that the original idol could be hidden somewhere due to recurring attacks of Moghul troops which occurred during the Bhoi rule. The presence of Vaishnava images like Nrusingha, Varaha and Trivikrama in subsidiary niches provides the impression that it was probably a Vaishnava Temple. Some of the loose sculptures of this temple are also found scattered around the temple premises. The temple is devoid of any decorative stone works over its walls. It is an east facing two chambered architecture having a rectangular Vimana and a Jagamohana. The Jagamohana has two entrances facing east & south. The temple structure is rectangular on plan and triangabada in elevation. The construction materials used are laterite and sandstone. The temple is in a very neglected state now. Wild trees and unkempt vegetation have grown all over the shikhara causing a big threat for its survival if not preserved at the earliest.

Tipuri Hero-Stones

There was information about a large depository of ancient Hero-stones lying neglected near a rice field of Tipuri village of Odisha. The Kanas region was earlier known to be 'Sirai Dandapata' during the Eastern Ganga era. The military importance of this region was significant. Presumably, a war was fought here during Eastern Ganga era (11th/12th Century AD). The region was under the control of the Somavamsi rulers earlier, when Eastern Ganga King Rajaraja and later his son, the great Chodagangadeva tried to access control over Odisha. From the Dirghasi Stone inscriptions of Banapati to surrounding areas like Chandramapatapur, Nirakarapur, Gadakharada, Malisahi, Tipuri etc. all yield a huge number of Hero-stones found scattered all around.

These Hero-stones, war memorials are likely to have been erected in the memories of those battle-heroes who sacrificed their lives. Most of the heroes in these memorial stones are depicted with a sword and a shield that signifies their connections to the battle. Some Lingapuja miniature votive temples are also found scattered around the place. We not only documented the archaeological findings but also interacted with locals and tried to sensitize them about the importance of these Hero-stones.

Indian "hero-stones" which have been erected since

very old times in various regions, are a branch of the Bronze-age Eurasian tradition of anthropomorphic stelae. Indian memorial stones are the object not only of archaeological, but also of ethnological studies; Variants of this have been found in the Śatarudriya hymn of the Yajurveda and even in the Mahābhārata. All this establishes that the specific worldview of "pastoral heroism", which had originated in the Eurasian steppe-belt in the Early Bronze age, survived

in India over several millennia, existing side by side with the mainstream Vedic-Hindu complex of ideas.

Hero-stones hold significant cultural and historical importance in Odisha, as they commemorate the valour of local heroes—often ordinary villagers—who sacrificed their lives for their communities. These stones serve not only as memorials but also as symbols of collective memory and identity, reflecting the values of bravery and selflessness deeply ingrained in local traditions. Erected by family members or fellow villagers, hero-stones often feature inscriptions that narrate the heroic deeds of the individuals they honour, thereby fostering a sense of pride and continuity within the community. Additionally, they contribute to cultural tourism by attracting visitors interested in the rich heritage and stories encapsulated in these monuments, thus promoting local history and identity while supporting economic development through tourism.

Bimala Temple

Vimala temple is one of the Adi Shakti Peethas, located within the Jagannath Temple complex in Puri, Odisha. Puri is not just one among the Char Dhams, but is also regarded as an abode of Goddess Vimala, and thus considered a Shakti Peetha. Goddess Vimala is regarded as the tantric consort of Lord Jagannath. Tantrics consider Jagannath as Shiva-Bhairava, rather than a form of Vishnu. It is believed that the feet (Pada Khanda) of Goddess Sati fell here. Sakta Tantric Jagannatha is Bhairava and Bimala is Bhairavi. She enjoys a dignified place in the Vaishnavite cult of Hindu mythology as 'Lakshmi'.

The relationship between Vimala and Lord Jagannath is rooted in Tantric Saivism and Shaktism, where Vimala is venerated as Bhairavi and Jagannath as Bhairava. The transformation of the bhogas (offerings) into Mahaprasad after being offered to Goddess Vimala illustrates her integral role in the religious practices. Additionally, Herman Kulke's research highlights Jagannath's connection to Ajaikapada Bhairava, as depicted in Konark temple carvings. This chapter explores these aspects and situates them within the broader tantric traditions of Puri.

The Jagannath Temple in Puri, one of the most significant pilgrimage sites in India, is deeply rooted in both Vaishnavism and Tantra. While much attention is given to the Vaishnavite elements of the temple, the Tantric aspects, particularly those involving Goddess Vimala, remain equally important yet less frequently discussed. Goddess Vimala, also known as Shreekshetrasvari (the goddess of the sacred land of Puri), plays a pivotal role in the temple's rituals, reflecting the Tantric synthesis in Jagannath worship.

Goddess Vimala in Tantric Tradition

According to Tantra Chudamani, Goddess Vimala is identified as Bhairavi, the consort of Bhairava, and Lord Jagannath is revered in the form of Bhairava. The tantric traditions at Puri emphasize this divine pairing, situating the Jagannath Temple as a centre of both Shaivism and Shaktism. The verse Odresu Vimala Saktin Jagannathastu Bhairavah highlights this relationship, portraying Jagannath as Bhairava and Vimala as his Shakti, underscoring the Tantric underpinnings of their worship (Kulke, 1980).

Transformation of Bhoga into Mahaprasad

One of the most fascinating aspects of the temple's rituals is the transformation of bhoga (food offerings) into Mahaprasad. The offerings to Lord Jagannath are considered ordinary until they are presented to Goddess Vimala, after which they become Mahaprasad—sacred food. This unique ritual practice signifies the vital role of the goddess in the daily life of the temple. It reflects the tantric belief in the power of Shakti, where even the most mundane objects (in this case, food) are transformed into something sacred after being blessed by the goddess (Chaudhuri, 1994).

Tantric Iconography: Ajaikapada Bhairava

The depiction of Jagannath as Ajaikapada Bhairava, particularly on a sculptural panel in the Konark Sun Temple, further illustrates the connection between Jagannath and Tantric Saivism. Herman Kulke, a scholar of the Jagannath cult, emphasizes that this iconography is not accidental but reflects the deep-rooted Tantric practices that were prevalent in Puri (Kulke, 1980). The representation of Ajaikapada Bhairava, a fierce form of Lord Shiva, links Jagannath to the Bhairava tradition, affirming his role as a Tantric deity within the broader context of Puri's religious landscape.

Puri as a Centre of Tantric Saivism and Shaktism

Historically, Puri has been a significant centre for Tantric Saivism and Shaktism. These esoteric traditions, which focus on the worship of Shiva and Shakti in their most potent and transformative forms, are integral to the

rituals of the Jagannath Temple. The temple's syncretic nature, combining Vaishnavite and Tantric elements, is epitomized by the dual worship of Jagannath as Bhairava and Vimala as Bhairavi (Chaudhuri, 1994). This fusion of traditions is also reflected in the architectural and ritualistic aspects of the temple, which continue to attract devotees from across different sects.

The role of Goddess Vimala in the Jagannath Temple, particularly in the context of Tantric rituals, cannot be overstated. As Bhairavi to Jagannath's Bhairava, she is central to the tantric practices that underlie the temple's rituals, especially in the transformation of bhoga into Mahaprasad. The depiction of Jagannath as Ajaikapada Bhairava further cements his connection to Tantric Saivism. Puri, as a historical center of tantric practices, continues to preserve these ancient traditions, making the Jagannath Temple a unique blend of Vaishnavism and Tantra.

Goddess Vimala is four handed image of chlorite stone, holding naga keyura and human figures in the upper hands and kalasa or Madyapatra and rosary in lower hands. A pronounced influence of tantric rites can be observed in the Yantra of Purusottama. The Yantra consists of an eight petalled lotus with the Vijamantra "klim" in the centre. The priests of Lord Jagannath temple first propitiate Lord Purusottama with goddess Lakshmi and then worship eight Saktis of Vishnu, namely Vimala, Utkarsini, Yajna, Kriya, Yoga, Prathvi, Satya and Isana. Vimala is regarded as one of the eight

Chandis of Purusottama Kshetra. The other seven Chandis are Ramachandi, Herachandi, Baselichandi, Alamchandi, Dakshinachandi and Jhadesvari. In the traditional rites Vimala is invoked as the Maya Shakti of Jagannath, Kriya Shakti of Balabhadra and Ichha Shakti of

Subhadra. She is regarded as the consort of Balabhadra. Source: (P.Singh, Pics: Unnikrishnan)

References
- Chaudhuri, S. (1994). Tantric Traditions in Odisha. New Delhi: Oxford University Press.
- Kulke, H. (1980). The Cult of Jagannath and the Regional Tradition of Orissa. New Delhi: Manohar.
- Mishra, S. (2000). Rituals and Traditions of the Jagannath Temple. Bhubaneswar: Jagannath Studies.

Dakshinakali Temple

Located at ten kms from Puri, this temple is famous for the belief of devotees on the profound blessings of Kali, the revered deity. Several Sakta temples are located inside, and outside Jagannath temple and Puri is considered as a centre of Vaishnavism as well as a Shakti Peetha. This temple is a Sakta temple dedicated to goddess Kali. There are various versions regarding the origin of the name Dakshina Kali. "Dakshinaa" refers to the gift given to a priest before performing a ritual or to one's guru. Such gifts are traditionally given with the right hand. Dakshinakali's two right hands are usually depicted in gestures of blessing and bestowing boons. Another version of the origin of her name comes from the story of Yama, lord of death, who resides in the south (dakshina). When Yama heard Kali's name, he fled in terror, and so those who worship Kali are said to be able to overcome death itself.

The temple is in the Biragobindapur village which nestles amidst lush green coconut trees and ponds filled with blooming lily flowers. It significantly contributes to the earnings of local service providers who cater to devotees and tourists. Local service providers, including priests, cooks, and vendors, earn income by offering services such as conducting rituals, preparing and selling prasad (offerings), and providing accommodation or transportation for visitors.

The Dakshina Kali temple attracts a steady flow of tourists, which enhances local business opportunities. Service providers benefit from increased foot traffic as visitors seek local cuisine, handicrafts, and lodging. This influx can lead to higher sales for local shops and food. The Temple serves as a community hub where people gather for festivals and events. The presence of this temple has led to better infrastructure in the village, such as roads, electricity, and water supply.

The festivals and religious ceremonies organized by the temple draws large crowds, providing villagers with opportunities to earn through various means such as food stalls, merchandise sales, and service offerings during these events. Village temples play a crucial role in enhancing the economic landscape of rural villages by providing diverse income opportunities for service providers through direct services, tourism, infrastructure development, and cultural engagement. This symbiotic relationship not only supports

individual livelihoods but also fosters community cohesion and economic resilience.

Despite her seemingly terrifying form, Kali Ma is often considered the kindest and most loving of all the Hindu goddesses, as she is regarded by her devotees as the mother of the whole Universe. And because of her form, she is also often seen as a great protector.

The *Chamunda Tantra* is a revered text within the *Tantra Shastra* tradition, focusing on the worship and the theological aspects of Chamunda, a fierce aspect of the goddess Durga. This text includes elaborate rituals, iconography, and metaphysical explanations related to various aspects of goddess worship, particularly emphasizing the ten powerful forms collectively known as the *Dasamahavidya*. These ten goddesses—Kali, Tara, Sodashi (Tripura Sundari), Bhubanesvari, Bhairavi, Chhinnamasta, Matangi, Kamala, Dhumavati, and Bagalamukhi—each represent distinct cosmic powers and serve unique spiritual purposes.

Overview of Chamunda Tantra

The *Chamunda Tantra* belongs to a class of Tantric texts that surfaced and gained prominence during the medieval period, coinciding with the rise of the *Shakta* tradition, which worships the Divine Feminine as the ultimate reality. The text is deeply rooted in esoteric philosophies and uses language rich with symbolism, often detailing methods for invoking and appeasing specific aspects of the Divine Mother.

According to the *Chamunda Tantra*, the goddess Chamunda herself embodies fierce, protective energy and presides over the cycle of destruction and rebirth. She is often depicted in a fearsome form, with elements that symbolize the stripping away of illusions and ego—a central theme in Tantric worship.

Dasamahavidya: The Ten Forms of the Goddess

The *Dasamahavidya*, or the "Ten Great Wisdoms," is a unique concept within the *Chamunda Tantra*. Each of these ten goddesses represents a different aspect of cosmic energy, with a particular focus on understanding and overcoming the dualities of life (such as birth-death, creation-destruction). The ten goddesses have the following symbolic significance:

- **Kali** - The fierce mother who embodies the concept of time and ultimate transformation.
- **Tara** - The guiding star, symbolizing knowledge and compassion.
- **Sodashi (Tripura Sundari)** - Representing supreme beauty and the power of desire.
- **Bhubanesvari** - The ruler of the universe, embodying the cosmic space.
- **Bhairavi** - The warrior goddess, associated with the aggressive aspects of reality.

- **Chhinnamasta** - Symbolizing self-sacrifice and the cyclical nature of life and death.
- **Dhumavati** - Representing the smoke, or void, after destruction.
- **Bagalamukhi** - A goddess of suppression, symbolizing the power to paralyze and still enemies.
- **Matangi** - The outcaste goddess, representing the marginalized aspects of society and wisdom.
- **Kamala** - Often identified with Lakshmi, symbolizing abundance and prosperity.

Iconography and Symbolism

The *Chamunda Tantra* provides detailed descriptions of each goddess, along with her iconography and associated symbols. For example:

- **Kali** is portrayed as dark-skinned, naked, with her tongue out, and wearing a garland of skulls. Her form is said to embody the cycle of creation and dissolution.
- **Chhinnamasta**, literally the "severed head," is depicted holding her own head while blood streams from her neck to signify sacrifice and transformation.
- **Bagalamukhi** is shown halting enemies with one hand, symbolizing her power to stop negative forces.

The *Chamunda Tantra* also gives intricate ritualistic details for worshiping these deities, often involving yantras (sacred diagrams), mantras, and mudras (hand gestures) unique to each form. The rituals are intended to invoke specific energies and achieve outcomes, whether spiritual enlightenment or practical blessings.

Tulaja Tantra describes eight forms of Kali - Dakshina Kali, Siddhi Kali, Guhya Kali, Sri Kali, Bhadra Kali, Chamunda Kali, Smasana Kali and Mahakali.

The Mahakali Samhita gives the names of nine forms of Goddess Kali - Dakshina Kali, Bhadra Kali, Smasana

Kali, Kalakali, Guhya Kali, Kamakali, Dhana Kali, Chandi Kali. Nine forms of Kali as described in the Tantrasara and Agamatatvavilasa are: Dakshina Kali, Maha Kali, Smasana Kali, Guhya Kali, Bhadrakali, Chamunda Kali, Siddha Kali, Hamsa Kali and Kamakala Kali. The images of Kali are depicted less in temple walls in comparision to Mahisamardini images. Elizabeth Harding in her book Kali: The Black Goddess of Dakshineswar states that "Hindus have many Gods and Goddesses, each evoking one aspect of divinity; so it is impossible to believe in an absolute entity or to believe in one form of God. Different gods and goddesses symbolize unique aspects. Goddess Kali has a ferocious appearance, in her glistening black or dark texture along with unruly, dishevelled hair. Kali

can be represented in many forms - as a playful child, a voluptuous woman, a warrior, or even a decrepit old hag. As a young woman, she is in the form of mother goddess. As a warrior, she is a defender, preserver, or a destroyer. An image of Kali is in the premises of Dhavalesvara Shiva temple near Cuttack. Seated in the Lalita pose on a lotus under which a corpse can be seen. In her right hand she holds a rosary and a sword in her uplifted back hand. Her right middle arm as well as all the left arms are broken. She wears a Kirita-mukuta and possesses a third eye.

The ancient Tantric texts have glorified Ekamra Kshetra as a Shakti-Pitha, a seat of the worship of the Devi. The Jnanarnava Tantra contains information relating to the Shri Vidya tradition and has detailed information on inner worship, rather than the external rituals (bahiryaga). Jnanarnava means Ocean of Knowledge. The "Swarnadrimahodaya" states that four Chandikas were enshrined at the corners of the Bindusagara. Two of these are the images of the Chamunda. The first image is found at the "jagamohana" of the Uttareshwar temple. The second one is the presiding deity of the Mohini temple.

Indralath Temple

A unique structure made entirely in brick that is one of the tallest temples in Odisha is the Indralath Temple. This majestic temple in Ranipur Jharial is one of the few surviving brick temples in India. Legend has it that the original Shiva Linga was worshipped by Lord Indra who then built this temple in his honour. It is a rare brick temple, described by different researchers and historians as either a Siva or Vishnu temple. Considered to be the tallest temple in Odisha, it is one of the few surviving ancient temples of Balangir, Odisha. The Shikhara, almost 60 feet high is erected on a high sand – stone platform. In the temple there are distinct images of Shiva-Parvati, Ganesh etc. The water channel tapering out from the linga is considered to be the original one.

This rare brick structure is a symbol of the great architectural skills of the craftsmen of South Kosala. Perched atop an elevated platform, it is a towering edifice, probably the highest brick temple among its prototypes in the upper Mahanadi valley in ancient South Kosala. The bricks which are used in this temple are generally 14 inches in length, seven inches in breadth. Cuboid in size, these bricks are well designed and strong. Pancharatha in style of architecture it consists of a vimana and a Jagamohana. The garbhagriha stands supported by four stone pillars in its four corners. The ceiling is carved with a beautifully designed lotus on the inner roof of the temple. Sculptural carving of the lotus on the ceiling of this temple not only magnifies its beauty but also adds to its religious importance as a sacred symbol. The superb masonry skills exhibit the advanced scientific techniques in architecture. The Indralath brick temple of Ranipur is truly a gem of the cultural excellence of South Kosala.

The Indralath Temple holds historical and cultural significance as one of the earliest Brahmanical temples in Odisha. It is believed to date back to the 7th or 8th century AD, attributed to Queen Vasata. This temple, with its prominent vertical stance and isolation, is a major tourist attraction and a subject of archaeological interest.

The sanctum, or garbhagriha, measures 8 feet 4 inches square and is accessible through an inner doorway of 3 feet 2 inches in width by 6 feet 4 inches in height. The outer doorway measures slightly smaller, at 3 feet 2 inches by 6 feet 1 inch. Supporting the structure are four sturdy pillars, placed at each corner of the garbhagriha, which showcase the structural strength and stylistic grandeur of early Odisha temple architecture. This Pancharatha-style temple reflects later developments in temple design. The

exterior walls feature niches measuring 1 foot 11 inches by 3 feet 4 inches on three sides, and these niches house rich sculptural elements that emphasize both Brahmanical and Buddhist influences. Notably, the garbhagriha ceiling is intricately carved with lotus motifs, which are also found at the entrance of the antarala, creating a cohesive artistic narrative within the temple.

The temple showcases a blend of iconographic elements from both Vaishnavism and Saivism, as well as Buddhist influences. High-relief sculptures on monolithic stone slabs include a Buddha image, hinting at the religious plurality of the period. Furthermore, six Naga pillars adorn the sanctum walls, arranged in pairs on the south, west, and north sides, suggesting a connection to Saivite traditions.

On the temple's three floors, windows with niches evoke the appearance of Buddhist chaitya halls, containing images of Varaha, Hanuman, and Nrisimha. The exterior walls also feature sculptures of significant Hindu deities and mythological scenes, such as Krishna subduing Kaliya and Hanuman carrying the Gandhamardana hill. Additionally, the presence of Ardhanarishvara, Vishnu incarnations (including Varaha and Nrisimha), and Sivalinga within the temple reflects the temple's syncretic religious orientation. While primarily a Vishnu temple, the Indralath Temple houses a Sivalinga and several images of Ganesha, Parvati, and Kanika within its sanctum, indicating a blend of religious traditions. The temple serves as a rare instance where a Siva temple is dedicated to Vishnu, reflecting the complexity of religious affiliations during the Somavamsi period. Scholar J.D. Beglar identifies the Indralath Temple as one of the oldest temples within the Ranipur-Jharial complex, suggesting a construction date in the 7th or 8th century AD.

Pataneswari Temple

The Pataneswari Temple in Patnagarh, located in the Bolangir district of Odisha is a significant historical and religious site dedicated to the goddess Pataneswari, a manifestation of Durga. This ancient temple, renowned for its architectural heritage, is intertwined with the rich history of the region, the cultural legacy of the Chauhan dynasty, and the religious traditions of Shakti worship. The temple not only serves as a place of worship but also as a cultural and historical artifact that has attracted the attention of scholars, historians, and devotees alike.

Pataneswari Temple is situated around 40 kms from Balangir at Patnagarh, the ancient capital of the Kingdom of Patna. Patnagarh today is a unique combination of a mytsic past and vibrant present. Steeped in natural beauty, this town is famous for many ancient temples. The shrine of Goddess Pataneswari, the presiding deity is reminiscent of the earliest group of temples built during the Chauhan rule in the western part of Odisha. The temple was built by Ramai Dev, the first Chauhan King of Western Odisha. The Devi here is enshrined in the form of ten-armed Mahishasuramardini holding war weapons including sword and shields, bow and arrow, thunderbolt, a snake and a long trident. This temple is also known as one of the Shakti Peetha's in Odisha.

Historical Background:

The Pataneswari Temple is believed to have been constructed during the 12th century under the patronage of the Chauhan dynasty, who ruled Patnagarh and much of Western Odisha. Historically known as the capital of the Chauhan's, Patnagarh served as a centre for administration, culture, and religion. The Chauhan rulers, who were ardent devotees of Shakti (the Divine Mother), contributed significantly to the construction of temples and supported the growth of Hinduism, especially the Shakta (goddess-centred) tradition.

The temple architecture exhibits influence of both Kalinga and Rajputana styles, symbolizing a confluence of local Odia culture and northern Indian influences. This syncretism is reflected in its carvings, structural layout, and unique decorative elements that combine iconography from Hindu, Jain, and folk traditions.

Before the arrival of the Chauhan rulers in the Patnagarh region, the area was a significant stronghold of Saivism and Tantric traditions. This influence is most notably seen in the religious centre of Ranipur-Jharial, home to a unique open-air (hypaethral) temple dedicated to the sixty-four Yoginis, as well as the renowned Somesvara Siva temple. The Somesvara temple, which houses an inscription bearing the name of Ganga Sivacharya, reflects the influence of the Mattamayura school of Saivism—a prominent sect that flourished during that period. This school's presence underscored Ranipur-Jharial's importance as a regional hub for Shaiva and Tantric practices.

However, with the advent of the Chauhan dynasty, significant changes took place in religious practices, though without undermining existing beliefs. The Chauhans introduced their own faith and practices but showed a remarkable tolerance for the local religious landscape. Ramai Deva, the first chief of the Chauhan dynasty, revered Asapuri Devi, the ancestral goddess worshipped by Chauhans across India. Instead of imposing her worship upon the locals, he respectfully embraced the existing traditions by declaring Asapuri Devi as "Pataneswari," the presiding deity of Patnagarh. This name change effectively aligned his family's tutelary goddess with the local religious identity, merging Chauhan lineage worship with the spiritual fabric of Patnagarh. Furthermore, Ramai Deva honoured the established local deities, ensuring their continued reverence. Kosaleswara Siva, who was previously the principal deity of Patnagarh, remained prominent under Chauhan rule. In fact, his temple was strategically positioned within the fort's premises, close to the shrine of Pataneswari, illustrating a harmonious coexistence of faiths within the kingdom.

This spirit of religious accommodation continued with Balarama Deva, a later Chauhan ruler who expanded the kingdom to the Sambalpur region. Like Ramai Deva, Balarama Deva embraced the local traditions, accepting the deity Samalai as the regional protector. He integrated her into the Chauhan family's spiritual practices by identifying her with his family's tutelary goddess. This alignment further exemplifies the Chauhans' strategy of blending their inherited beliefs with local faiths, allowing them to establish legitimacy and rapport with their subjects.

The Chauhans were adherents of the Pancha Devata (Five Divinities) tradition, which emphasizes worship of a group of five primary deities: Vishnu, Shiva, Durga, Surya, and Ganesha. This approach allowed the Chauhans to connect with a wide range of local spiritual traditions, as these deities were widely revered throughout the region.

In addition to mainstream deities, lesser-known and esoteric sects, such as the Kurmbhipatia and Kabirpanthi faiths, were also practiced within the Chauhan kingdom. These sects, known for their unique practices and often mystical outlooks, added to the region's diverse religious landscape, reflecting an inclusive spiritual environment under Chauhan rule.

Thus, the Chauhans of Patnagarh skillfully balanced their religious devotion to family deities with the spiritual traditions of their subjects, cultivating a pluralistic kingdom where both imported and indigenous beliefs could coexist. This nuanced integration of Shaivism, Shaktism, and other lesser-known religious traditions enriched the cultural and spiritual heritage of Patnagarh, creating a vibrant legacy that resonates to this day.

The Goddess Pataneswari: Attributes and Significance

Pataneswari is a fierce form of Goddess Durga, embodying both the nurturing and warrior aspects of the Divine Feminine. She is regarded as the protector of Patnagarh and is revered as a guardian deity who safeguards her devotees from harm. The name "Pataneswari" translates to "Goddess of Patana (Patnagarh)," symbolizing her role as the spiritual custodian of the region. The image of Pataneswari is an example of Odisha's unique iconography, where she combines the maternal and fearsome qualities of the Divine Feminine. Pataneswari, is also associated with fertility, protection, and empowerment, making her a central figure in the spiritual lives of the local populace.

The Pataneswari Temple's architecture reflects the distinctive Kalinga style characterized by elaborate rekha deula, ornate carvings, and intricate motifs. The inner sanctum, or garbhagriha, houses the deity and is the core area of the temple.

The Pataneswari Temple is not only a centre for Shakti worship but also serves as a focal point for cultural festivals and events. The temple holds special significance during the Dussehra festival, where the goddess is adorned in elaborate attire and worshipped as a manifestation of Durga. This celebration draws devotees from various parts of Odisha and neighbouring states, illustrating the temple's status as a spiritual and cultural hub.

Festivals and Rituals

Dussehra: This festival celebrates the triumph of good over evil and is marked by elaborate rituals, processions, and special offerings to the goddess.

Chaitra Navratri: During the nine days of Navratri, the temple witnesses an influx of devotees who participate in the recitations, fasting, and worship dedicated to Pataneswari.

Daily Worship and Offerings: Traditional rituals involve offering rice, fruits, and sweets, symbolizing gratitude and devotion.

Pataneswari Temple and Shakti Tradition

The goddess Pataneswari is central to the Shakti tradition within Odisha. The Shakti sect, one of the most ancient branches of Hinduism, emphasizes the worship of feminine power or energy (Shakti) and regards the goddess as the ultimate reality. The Pataneswari Temple plays an important role in sustaining this tradition by providing a sacred space for the followers of Shakti worship, particularly those drawn to the fierce and protective aspects of the goddess.

The Pataneswari Temple is an embodiment of Odisha's cultural heritage, encapsulating centuries of religious devotion, architectural brilliance, and artistic expression. For the people of Patnagarh and beyond, it remains a testament to the enduring presence of goddess worship in daily life and cultural practices. As one of the oldest temples in the region, it stands as a monument to the devotional fervour of the past and continues to inspire contemporary worshippers with its spiritual and historical resonance.

References

- Mishra, S. C. (1983). Cultural Heritage of Odisha. Cuttack: Odisha Historical Review.
- Patnaik, N. (2001). Odishan Temples: Architecture

and Iconography. New Delhi: Rupa Publications.
- Sharma, H. D. (2015). A Study of Shakti Worship in India. New Delhi: Shakti Publications.
- Department of Culture, Government of Odisha. (2023). Temples of Western Odisha: An Overview. Bhubaneswar: Odisha State Archaeology.

Ancient Jain Idols

Koraput, a district in Odisha, India, is renowned for its scenic landscapes and the diverse cultural heritage of its tribal communities. Less known, however, is its significant Jain legacy, evident through ancient idols and temples across various sites, particularly in Kechela, Nandapur, Subai, and Bisingpur. This region, once a seat of Jain activity, retains invaluable relics that mark the influence of Jainism in medieval Odisha. Kechela, located on the southern bank of the Kolab river, is one of the foremost sites with well-preserved Jain sculptures that reflect the area's historical religious diversity.

Kechela: A Historical Site of Jain Significance

Kechela is located approximately 10 kilometres from Koraput and has ancient Jain images, including representations of Lord Rishabnath, Lord Mahavir, Ambika Devi, Yaksha, and Yakshini. The sculptures display a high degree of artistic sophistication, hinting at a flourishing Jain community and advanced craftsmanship in the region. Scholars have associated these idols with the medieval period due to the stylistic details and iconographic features that align with Jain traditions from that era (Patnaik, 1989).

The presence of both male and female deities (Yaksha and Yakshini) alongside prominent Tirthankaras suggests the importance of Yaksha cults in medieval Jain worship, a common feature in Jain temples across ancient India (Shah, 2004). This indicates that the Jain community in Kechela and surrounding areas might have been substantial, with developed traditions and rituals unique to the region.

Jain Heritage Across Koraput and Neighbouring Areas

Apart from Kechela, other locations in Koraput, such as Nandapur, Jamunda, Kotpad, Jeypore, and Borrigumma, house notable Jain relics. The idols are often found in the form of Tirthankaras, votive tablets, Yakshas,

and Yakshinis, some of which have been repurposed within Hindu temples. Scholars argue that the migration of Jain artifacts into Hindu worship spaces highlights a process of syncretism, whereby Jain deities were venerated as Hindu gods, such as Bhairavas and Gramadevatas (local village deities), blending Jain and Hindu cultural elements (Behera, 2001).

Koraput is noted to have the highest concentration of ancient Jain statues in Odisha. These sites likely played a key role in disseminating Jain philosophies and practices during the region's medieval period, as evidenced by inscriptions and the stylistic elements of sculptures. The distinctive iconography and artistic techniques in these idols offer critical insights into the local adaptations of Jain art forms, as well as the spread of Jain ideals in eastern India (Mohanty, 1997).

Integration of Jain Artifacts into Hindu Worship

Interestingly, many of the Jain idols in Odisha, including those from Koraput, have been repurposed and incorporated into Hindu temples. This phenomenon aligns with similar practices observed across India, where Jain sculptures have found new religious significance within Hindu contexts. This cultural integration of Jain deities as Hindu figures speaks to the fluid nature of religious boundaries in India and the resilience of ancient religious artifacts (Agarwal, 2008). For example, Tirthankaras are often worshipped as Bhairavas in local Hindu temples, and female deities like Ambika Devi are revered as village goddesses. Such practices not only ensure the preservation of these ancient relics but also reflect the dynamic interplay of religious identities in Odisha.

Implications for Heritage Conservation

The Jain relics in Koraput are valuable to both historians and conservationists for their insights into religious dynamics and local craftsmanship. However, the repurposing of Jain artifacts within Hindu worship poses challenges for preserving the original religious context of these idols. Current heritage preservation efforts may need to consider the dual religious identities of these artifacts, aiming to protect the idols while respecting the contemporary cultural practices surrounding them. Preservation initiatives that document and display these artifacts with both Jain and Hindu histories could promote a more inclusive understanding of Odisha's religious heritage, showcasing the cultural and religious pluralism that has characterized the region across centuries.

The ancient Jain idols and temples of Koraput, particularly the site at Kechela, bear testimony to the once-thriving Jain community in Odisha. Through exquisite craftsmanship and historical richness, these relics highlight

the cultural confluence and religious fluidity that define the region. The integration of Jain idols into Hindu worship contexts presents both a challenge and an opportunity for heritage conservation, underscoring the need for approaches that honour the multi-layered heritage of Koraput.

References
- Agarwal, R. (2008). Syncretism in Religious Art: Jain and Hindu Idols in Odisha. Indian Art Journal, 15(2), 102-118.
- Behera, A. (2001). Religious Syncretism in Medieval Odisha: Jain and Hindu Influences. Bhubaneswar: Odisha Historical Press.
- Mohanty, S. (1997). Iconography and Symbolism in Jain Art of Eastern India. Cultural Studies Quarterly, 9(1), 56-67.
- Patnaik, M. (1989). The Art and Architecture of Odisha: Jain and Buddhist Influences. Cuttack: Utkal University Press.
- Shah, U.P. (2004). Yaksha Cults and the Evolution of Jain Worship. Journal of Indian Art and Archaeology, 20(3), 203-221.

The Twin Temples of Gandharadi

Siddhesvara and Nilamadhava Temples

The twin temples of Siddhesvara and Nilamadhava at Gandharadi are unique architectural marvels from early medieval Odisha, dedicated to Lord Siva and Lord Vishnu, respectively. Their strategic construction on a shared platform and distinctive stylistic elements provides an essential link in understanding the evolution of Odisha's temple architecture. This chapter delves into the historical background, architectural features, religious significance, and cultural heritage of the Gandharadi temples. Additionally, it highlights the influence of the Bhanja dynasty, under whose aegis these temples were constructed, shedding light on their role in fostering religious and architectural syncretism.

Gandharadi, located in the ancient Khinjali-mandala region of the upper Mahanadi valley, houses the remarkable Siddhesvara and Nilamadhava temples. This ancient site was under the rule of the Bhanja dynasty during the early medieval period. Built on a unified platform, the temples exemplify the dual worship of Siva and Vishnu, a theme prominent in the religious history of Odisha. The region of Gandharadi fell under the sovereignty of the Bhanjas, feudatories who owed allegiance to the Bhauma-karas. Known for their architectural contributions, the Bhanjas asserted their independence during the period of Bhauma turmoil, as evidenced by inscriptions found in copperplate grants. Notably, during the reign of Maharaja Vidyadarabhanja and his son Nettabhanja II, the Bhanjas took on an autonomous role in supporting the last rulers of the Bhauma-kara dynasty. The region was later annexed by Yayati I Mahasivagupta in his quest to consolidate Utkala under his rule. The Siddhesvara and Nilamadhava temples share a platform, or pitha, and are of the rekha order with flat-roofed jagamohanas (halls) that exhibit several distinctive architectural features.

Siddhesvara Temple (Dedicated to Siva)

The presiding deity of the Siddhesvara temple is a Sivalingam situated within a square yonipitha crafted from chlorite stone. The temple hosts annual festivals such as Sivaratri, Kartika Purnima, Sravana Somavara, and Danda Yatra. The sikhara of the temple is adorned with a Sivalinga, symbolizing its dedication to Siva. In addition to Siddhesvara, other significant deities are found in nearby shrines, such as Kapilesvara and Paschima Somanath. Nearby, a beautiful yet weather-worn image of eight-armed Durga, worshipped under a banyan tree, suggests that these ancient figures once adorned the main sanctum.

Nilamadhava Temple (Dedicated to Vishnu)

The Nilamadhava temple houses a four-armed Vishnu in a samabhanga pose. The deity stands on a shallow platform flanked by Sridevi and Bhudevi, who are considered embodiments of prosperity and the earth. Vishnu is adorned with a kirita mukuta (crown) and a vanamala (garland of leaves) draped over the shoulder. At the apex of the idol, two flying Vidyadharas are depicted holding garlands, enhancing the divine atmosphere. The temple's sikhara is surmounted by a Wheel (Chakra) crafted from blue chlorite stone, affirming its dedication to Vishnu.

The Platform and Jagamohana Construction

Both temples are built on a raised platform embellished with pabhaga mouldings and jangha decorated with miniature mundis and pilasters. Each side of the platform includes small corner shrines, adhering to the pancayatana layout. The roofs of the jagamohanas are constructed using the cantilever principle, originally supported by twelve large pillars arranged in a square pattern. Over time, these openings were enclosed using ashlar masonry and latticework to strengthen the structure. Notably, the ornamentation is minimal, offering an insight into the aesthetic transitions within the Odishan temple architecture.

The twin temples are among the earliest surviving examples of a dual temple complex dedicated to both Siva and Vishnu. This architectural syncretism, evident in structures like Simhanatha and Baidyanath temples, underscores the region's cultural accommodation of multiple sects. Such dual worship represents an essential characteristic of Odisha's religious history, where followers of Siva and Vishnu often shared temple spaces, fostering inter-sect harmony. The Gandharadi temples are an important phase in the Odishan temple architectural style, particularly notable for their simplified ornamentation. While other temples in Odisha showcase complex decorative styles with intricate carvings, Gandharadi's restrained design highlights the transition towards more elaborate ornamentation in later periods. The stylized chaitya windows, pilaster bases, and jagamohana simplicity reflect early Odishan styles, anticipating the decorative complexity that would emerge in the 10th and 11th centuries in coastal Odisha.

The Role of the Bhanja Dynasty in the Temple's Legacy

The Bhanjas, who governed Khinjali-mandala, made significant contributions to the architectural and religious development of the region. Their alliance with the Bhauma-kara dynasty, especially through familial ties, underscored their political and cultural influence. Later, under pressure from Yayati I Mahasivagupta, the Bhanjas reverted to a feudatory status. Yet, their legacy in promoting religious tolerance through shared worship sites remained influential, as evidenced by the Gandharadi temples.

Preservation and Archaeological Importance

Despite their historical importance, the Gandharadi temples face deterioration. The eight-armed Durga idol and other relics, exposed to the elements, reflect the challenges in preserving these early medieval sculptures. Continued archaeological work and conservation efforts are crucial to preserving these monuments that stand as testaments to Odisha's architectural innovation and religious pluralism. The Gandharadi temples of Siddhesvara and Nilamadhava are crucial to understanding early medieval temple architecture in Odisha. Built under the patronage of the Bhanjas, these temples represent a harmonious blend of religious ideologies, architectural styles, and minimalistic decorative programs that evolved into the grandiose designs seen in later Odishan temples. The Gandharadi complex is a monumental testament to the early stages of temple architecture in Odisha, with significant contributions to the heritage and cultural syncretism of the region.

References

- Boudh Plates of Ranabhanja.
- Taltali Copper-plate of Dharma Mahadevis.
- Copper-plate Grant of Yayati I Mahasivagupta (A.D. 935).
- International Journal of Novel Research and Development (IJNRD), Volume 9, Issue 3, 2024

Batrish Singhasan

The Batrish Singhasan is a rare and fascinating place in the town of Nandapur, situated in the Koraput district of Odisha, surrounded by lush green hills and a culture rooted in tribal traditions. This throne is not merely a relic but a cultural symbol, encapsulating the spirit of ancient Indian wisdom, folklore, and royal legacy.

The first time I had visited this site was during my schooldays. My father, as an engineer with the State Government, had frequent official tours to Koraput and had taken us all. We imbibed the love for travel during those days of never getting tired. Batrish Singhasan – a throne with a flight of 32 steps leading to it, akin to the famous Battisi Singhasan of King Vikramaditya of Ujjain, is a symbol of the rich cultural heritage of Nandapur village, Koraput. There are many tales & folklores about the origin of the site, popular among locals. "A herding community known as Goudas lived in Nandapur and its adjoining villages. A young Gouda cattle herder came across the hillock where Batrish Singhasan stands. He used this spot to sit and playfully deliver judgments like a scholar or a great king. However, once out of this place, his behaviour changed to that of a common man". (Prof Kapila Khemundu HoD, Department of Sociology, Central University, Koraput).

The legend of the Batrish Singhasan is closely linked to the Vikramaditya folklore, especially the tales of the magical throne that would speak to anyone who dared to sit on it without being as wise and virtuous as the king himself. According to these legends, the throne contains thirty-two statues or figurines, each said to contain a spirit that would pose moral and philosophical challenges to any unworthy individual who tried to ascend the throne. These statues, each representing a guardian or embodiment of wisdom, would test the righteousness of the person attempting to sit on the throne, reflecting the moral tenets of the time.

The tales around Vikramaditya's Batrish Singhasan form the basis of various folk stories known as the Singhasan Battisi. In these stories, King Bhoja, who ruled centuries after Vikramaditya, discovered the throne and attempted to sit on it. However, each time he tried, a statue would come to life and narrate a story illustrating Vikramaditya's wisdom and courage. Through these stories, Bhoja gained insights into righteous rule, indicating that only a monarch with an impeccable moral compass could sit upon the throne. In the context of Nandapur, the Batrish Singhasan holds an equally revered position. The locals regard it as a sacred relic, attributing mystical powers to the site. Stories are passed down orally, blending historical imagination with local belief, further enhancing the throne's status as a symbol of wisdom and justice.

Legend also has it that the King of Jeypore back from hunting in nearby forests, used this place as his throne. Sitting on this throne, he delivered judgements on public matters just like the legendary Vikramaditya. This led to the naming of this place. Few researchers also say that the historical throne is inextricably linked to Silavamsis who ruled over Vindhyas in 14th century. These rulers with their seat of administration at Nandapur – the first capital of the Jeypore Kingdom—tried to emulate the glory of

Vikramaditya of Ujjain. The Last Silavamsa ruler- Vinayak Deo, who ruled from 1443 AD as a Suryavamsi ruler claiming his descent from an ancient Rajput prince, had installed the throne known as Vikramarka which is still to be found there.

These days, Goddess Kanak Durga is worshipped as the main deity on the throne along with Ashta Betals. This historical structure is one of the 218 protected monuments of the Odisha State Archaeology and has been declared as a heritage site under the Ancient Monuments Preservation Act.

Subei Jain temples

The Subei Jain Temples, nestled in the hilly terrains of the Koraput district in Odisha, are among the most ancient remnants of Jainism in the state. These temples, which date back several centuries, illustrate the cultural interaction between Jainism and the tribal communities of Odisha, a region that is otherwise predominantly Hindu. The Subei Jain Temples are known not only for their spiritual heritage but also for their distinctive architecture and iconography, which reflect the artistic evolution of the Jain community. The temples offer a glimpse into an era when Jainism flourished in Odisha and contributed to the social and religious landscape of the region. In the present day, while Jainism is a minority faith in Odisha, the temples continue to be of significance to both pilgrims and researchers, as well as to the local communities who regard the monuments with reverence and as part of their heritage.

The temples are located close to Nandapur, around 40 kms from Koraput. One of the lesser-known destinations, it has great historical significance. We started for Subei in the afternoon and enjoyed the pleasant drive past Sunabeda. Memories of my past trips brought back special moments. As we approached the temple complex, we noticed a whitewashed Shiva temple close to it. Pillars and colourful flags were being put up for celebrating "Shivaratri". A young boy explained to us that the entire temple complex was housing Hindu Gods and Goddesses and not Jain Tirthankaras. I wondered at the loss of information that often happens with time, how history could be misrepresented.

In ancient times, the areas of the district formed part of the Dandaka Forest. The Jaina monuments of the village are noticed at the foot of the Panagiri hill. The temple was initially built with triratha architecture with amalaka. The door jabs have carvings of rosette enclosed with dotted squares. One temple is famous for its rare images of the tirthankaras. The temple houses an image of Rishabhanatha in padmasan dhyāna posture, surrounded by tirthankaras. The figures of the Trithankaras are depicted in sitting position on pedestals. The statues of the Tirthankaras are flanked by chauri bearers, Kevala tree, trilinear umbrella, Prabhamandala and flying Apsaras. The hair on the head of the figures are arranged in matted locks. Based on the architectural features, the temple can be assigned to the ninth century A.D. The temples are dedicated to Mahavira, Parshvanatha, Rishabhanatha and other Tirthankaras.

The Subei Jaina sculptures, particularly those of Risabhanatha, exhibit distinctive iconographic and stylistic elements across several shrines and images. Among the four main shrines, the two east-facing shrines each feature

an image of a Jaina Sasanadevi, while the west-facing shrines display one image of Risabhanatha and another shrine with three Risabhanatha figures. The iconography of these sculptures, detailed below, reveals significant insights into the artistic conventions and spiritual symbolism of the period.

Risabhanatha Images

Most images of Risabhanatha are carved seated in dhyanamudra on plain or lotus pedestals, typically featuring his lanchana, the bull, either on or beneath the pedestal. Risabhanatha's Sasanadevi, Chakresvari, is frequently depicted below the main figure, often flanked by spirited lions and kneeling devotees. In some depictions, Chakresvari sits atop a Garuda, with attributes such as a disc, varadamudra, mace, and vessel. The Tirthankara is distinguished by elongated earlobes, jata (matted hair) often draping over his shoulders, and a lotus-petal halo (prabhamandala) behind his head. Overhead, a trilinear umbrella and branches of the kevala tree represent enlightenment.

Vertical compositions typically include bedecked chauri bearers, flying gandharvas with garlands, and elephants, while the halo is often bordered by a beaded chain. Certain sculptures include additional iconographic features such as the auspicious srivatsa mark on the chest and trivali (three horizontal lines) on the neck, further symbolizing Risabhanatha's divine status. Notably, one Risabhanatha image integrates all 24 Tirthankaras surrounding the main figure, each with their respective lanchanas. These images at Subei are often embellished with elaborate pedestals featuring additional figures and sometimes include a pranala (drainage spout) for ritual offerings.

Mahavira Image

An image of Mahavira is carved similarly in dhyanamudra, accompanied by his Sasanadevi Sidhayika, who is seated below with four arms, holding a parasu, shula, and other symbolic objects. This sculpture shares characteristics such as a lotus-petal halo, trilinear umbrella, and chauri bearers flanking the central figure.

Notable Sasanadevis: Chakresvari, Rohini, and Ambika

Chakresvari, the Sasanadevi of Risabhanatha, appears in various forms, including a striking depiction with 16 arms holding objects like a mace, sword, and bow. She is represented with a conical crown and a halo decorated with lotus petals and astagrahas in a yogasana row.

Rohini, the Sasanadevi of Ajitanatha, is carved in dhyanamudra, flanked by kneeling devotees. Her iconography is unique, displaying items such as a vajra and tridandi, and features a Shivalinga-like object beneath her pedestal—an unusual element in Odisha's Jaina art.

Ambika, the Yakshi of Neminatha, is depicted seated in lalitasana on a double-petalled lotus with a lion below, holding a child in her lap and a bunch of mangoes, symbolizing fertility. A mango tree with the image of Neminatha at its summit and adorned by gandharvas completes the composition, which is marked by intricate jewellery and ornamental details. The sculptural ensemble at Subei offers a wealth of iconographic details significant to Jaina art. These images, particularly those of Risabhanatha, demonstrate a consistent iconographic program characterized by detailed halo design, kevala tree branches, trilinear umbrellas, and chauri bearers. They not only reflect the devotion of the period but also the refined sculptural aesthetics of Odisha's Jaina heritage.

Contemporary Relevance and Cultural Impact

Though Jainism is practiced by a small minority in Odisha today, the Subai Jain Temples remain culturally significant. They are visited by Jain pilgrims from various parts of India, particularly during auspicious Jain festivals such as Mahavir Jayanti. The temples also attract researchers and historians who study Odisha's religious pluralism and the influence of Jainism on the region. For the local communities in Koraput, the Subai temples have become part of their cultural identity. The tribal populations regard the temples with respect, seeing them as a link to their region's historical and religious diversity. The temples serve as a symbol of coexistence between different religious communities, as local festivals occasionally include elements honouring the Jain heritage.

In recent years, efforts have been made to preserve and promote these temples as part of Odisha's cultural heritage. The Odisha state government and the Jain community have initiated preservation projects to protect the temples from environmental and human-induced deterioration. The temples are being promoted as heritage tourism sites, drawing interest not only from Jain pilgrims but also from cultural enthusiasts, further enhancing the relevance of these ancient sites in the modern context. The spiritual messages embodied in the Subai temples, particularly the principles of non-violence, compassion, and respect for nature, resonate with contemporary concerns around environmental preservation and sustainable living. In a world increasingly aware of the need for ecological balance, the values represented by these temples provide timeless wisdom that transcends religious boundaries.

The Subai Jain Temples of Koraput are a remarkable testament to the rich religious tapestry of Odisha, where

Jainism found a foothold centuries ago and left an indelible mark. The temples' iconography and architecture reflect the adaptation of Jain principles within a local aesthetic framework, creating a unique blend of spiritual and artistic expression. Today, the temples stand not only as historical artifacts but as living symbols of interfaith harmony and respect for nature, carrying forward the values of compassion and peace espoused by Jainism. Preserving the Subai Jain Temples ensures that future generations can appreciate the diversity of Odisha's heritage and draw inspiration from Jain philosophy. These temples, with their peaceful surroundings and powerful iconography, continue to remind visitors of a time when religion and spirituality were seamlessly interwoven with art, culture, and daily life, offering timeless lessons on coexisting with nature and fostering peace in society.

Ambika Temple

The Ambika Temple, located in the village of Kenduli-Deuli in Odisha's Prachi Valley, is a notable example of Kalinga-style architecture and ancient Sakta tradition in the region. Kenduli is also celebrated as the birthplace of Jayadeva, the illustrious 12th-century poet-saint known for his Sanskrit masterpiece, the *Gita Govinda*. This temple, now under the protection of the Odisha State Archaeology Department, has undergone significant reconstruction in recent years, built upon the remains of an earlier structure thought to date back to the Ganga period (Mohapatra, 2017, p.411).

Architectural Features of the Temple

The Ambika Temple exhibits the typical structural elements of Kalinga architecture, with its two main sections: the vimana (sanctum tower) and jagamohana (assembly hall). Constructed primarily with laterite stones, sandstone, and a variety of burnt bricks, the temple faces east, following a traditional orientation. The vimana is of the pancharatha rekha deula style, standing approximately 35 feet high. The design is noted for its vertical bands on the central facade of each paga (offset) and a simple, two-molded *bandhana* on the *bada* (base). Additionally, the *baranda* of the *bada* contains a single, flat-shaped molding. The gandi, or superstructure, is pyramidal with five distinct *paga*s adorned with Jhapa Simha (protective lion figures), while the mastaka (top portion) includes elements such as the neck, ghanta (bell), amalakashila (cushion stone), and kalasa (finial pot).

The jagamohana is a pidha deula style hall, approximately 27 feet high (Mohapatra, 2011, p.66). It retains a pyramidal gandi with seven horizontal *pidha* (tiered roof) moldings and tankus (projecting nails) on all sides. Like the vimana, the jagamohana features a mastaka composed of neck, ghanta, amalakashila, khapuri (crown), and kalasa, though it lacks ayudha (weapon) and dhvaja (flag). Notably, the interior walls of the jagamohana remain unadorned, underscoring its austere design.

Iconography of the Deities

Central to the Ambika Temple is the presiding deity, Devi Ambika, whose image is a stunning exemplar of Odishan classical art from the Ganga period. The black chlorite stone statue, measuring 42 x 20 inches, portrays Ambika in *padmasana* (lotus posture) on a double-petaled lotus base. This icon displays Ambika with her right arm broken at the elbow and holding a cluster of five mangoes, while her left hand bears a lotus flower (Mohapatra, 2017, pp.412-413). The iconography of the image includes a lion figure and female devotees with musical instruments on the podium, showcasing the artistry of the Ganga dynasty. Above her head, a seven-hooded serpent and two apsara figures add to the elaborate detailing of the deity's image, which is said to embody the essence of Devi Chandi (Mohapatra, Vol. I, 1986, pp.126-127).

In addition to Ambika, the temple houses an image of Jagesvari, believed to be Padmavati by local tradition, although some scholars identify her as Jaina Vidyadevi

Jagesvari. Carved from black chlorite, Jagesvari sits in a meditative lotus posture, holding a fruit in her right hand and a lotus flower above her left arm. Her head is adorned by a seven-hooded serpent, with apsara figures crowning the stone slab. This depiction aligns with the artistic conventions of the Ganga period, emphasizing the symbolic and spiritual attributes of Jagesvari (Mohapatra, 2017, p.414).

Additional Features and Surroundings

The temple's sanctum doorway, though sparse in embellishment, includes dvarapalika (door guardians) and a carving of Gaja-Lakshmi on the lintel. Gaja-Lakshmi, seated in *lalitasana* (graceful posture), is flanked by two elephants pouring water from jars held in their trunks, symbolizing prosperity and blessings. Above the lintel, the Navagrahas (nine planetary deities) are displayed in *yogasana* (seated posture), each occupying a niche and holding symbolic elements (Mohapatra, 2017, p.413).

To the northeast of the main temple lies a Shaiva shrine dedicated to Lord Muktesvara Shiva. This smaller shrine, with a conical roof supported by stone pillars, holds a Shaktipitha (seat of the goddess) believed to enshrine a buried Shiva Lingam. Fragments of ancient stone pillars and other artifacts recovered from the temple site suggest the existence of a pillared mandapa (hall) that once enhanced the temple's architectural complexity (Mahapatra, 1997, p.10).

Evidence from inscriptions on a doorway lintel preserved in the Kenduli Museum places the original temple construction in the latter half of the 12th century A.D. During excavations, K.N. Mahapatra documented engravings reading "Jaya Jaya Deba Hare" alongside a

Hidden Heritage: The Lesser-Known Temples of Odisha | **115**

Saka-era date corresponding to 1190 A.D., indicating that the temple was established after the birth of Jayadeva and may have been contemporaneous with or following the composition of the *Gita Govinda* (Mahapatra, 1997, p.9). Additional details from T.E. Donaldson suggest that the original Ambika Temple belonged to the 13th century A.D., a view supported by architectural parallels found in Ganga-period monuments throughout Odisha (Donaldson, 1985/1986, Vol. II, p.687).

The temple's recent renovation, which began in the 20th century, preserved the ruins and incorporated modern materials, such as laterite stone and cement, to reconstruct the ancient vimana and jagamohana on their original bases. The re-erection of the Ambika Temple illustrates an enduring cultural dedication to preserving Odisha's architectural heritage and devotional sites (Mohapatra, 2017, p.415).

The Ambika Temple in Kenduli stands as an important witness to Odisha's religious and artistic history. Its iconography reflects the Sakta tradition's influence, while its architectural features highlight the distinctive Kalinga style that flourished during the Ganga dynasty. The temple, steeped in the spiritual legacy of the Prachi Valley, serves as a reminder of the region's ancient and ongoing reverence for Devi worship. Through preservation efforts and scholarly research, this temple continues to inspire a deeper understanding of Odisha's medieval architectural and cultural landscape.

Raghunath Temple

Jeypore, Odisha was the capital of the Surya Vamshi Kings who ruled this region for 508 years till 1952 when the estate was abolished. Descendants of the Solar Dynasty (Surya Vamshi) the kings- 'Kula Devata' was Lord Rama. The temple dedicated to the family God was constructed opposite to the palace. This temple is popularly known as Raghunath Temple, one of the oldest temples of Jeypore.

Jeypore, known as the "City of Victory," is situated in the southwestern region of Odisha, within the modern-day Koraput District, spanning an area of around 10,000 square miles. This vibrant city offers visitors not only untouched natural beauty—mountains, rivulets, and lush forests— but also a rich historical and cultural tapestry that dates back through the ages. Nestled in the scenic Eastern Ghats, Jeypore has long held the reputation of a jungle territory, yet its significance in the cultural heritage of Odisha is profound and remarkable. It embodies a unique fusion of Hindu, Jain, Buddhist, and tribal traditions, offering a captivating mix for culture enthusiasts. The area, relatively autonomous due to its remote location, developed a distinct identity influenced by a high concentration of tribal groups who shaped their religious and social customs around natural phenomena, harvest cycles, and deities represented by stones, pillars, and other simple forms.

This tribal kingdom integrated Hindu practices and

beliefs over time, driven in part by rulers who sought to unite their subjects under a shared religious and political system. They established tribal governance structures to preserve local customs while inviting Brahmins, merchants, and soldiers to introduce Hindu practices, creating a harmonious blend of tribal, Brahmanical, Jaina, and Buddhist elements. Evidence shows that religious leaders from various sects had attempted to Aryanize and integrate these regions well before the rulers' influence, indicating a longstanding history of cultural exchange.

One of Jeypore's most distinguished landmarks, the

Raghunath Temple, embodies this historical confluence. Situated in the heart of Jeypore, the temple is dedicated to Lord Raghunath (an incarnation of Lord Rama) and stands as a testament to the region's deep spiritual roots. The temple, with its intricate carvings and ornate architecture, exemplifies both local tribal artistry and traditional Hindu craftsmanship. It is believed that the Raghunath Temple was established by the local rulers, who sought to foster unity by creating a sacred space that embraced diverse cultural practices. The annual Rath Yatra festival celebrated here is an occasion of great festivity, drawing devotees from the entire region. During this time, the temple becomes the center of communal gatherings, reflecting the seamless interweaving of tribal and Hindu traditions that defines Jeypore's cultural landscape.

Narasimha Temple

Puri, a prominent Vaishnavite centre located in Odisha, holds a unique position in the religious history of India. Known as Srikshetra, Puri gained prominence not through political power but as a hub of socio-religious and cultural significance. Unlike many revered religious centres, Puri never served as a capital in Odisha's political history. Instead, its sanctity as a city of gods transcended the rise and fall of various dynasties, establishing it as a timeless pilgrimage destination. Historically, Puri has been associated with several deities, transforming from the "land of Narasimha" to "the land of Purusottama" and, ultimately, the "land of Lord Jagannath." Despite the lack of detailed historical records for Puri during the rule of early Odisha dynasties like the Chedis, Murundas, Matharas, Pitruvaktas, Vigrahas, Sailodvabas, and Bhaumakars, archaeological and literary references suggest that the site was regarded as a centre of religious importance. Early tribal worship of Madhava at Puri supports the notion that the region held spiritual significance well before the temple complex's construction.

Puri's religious identity has evolved over centuries, integrating various deities and traditions within its historical narrative. Its association with Narasimha, Purusottama, and eventually, Lord Jagannath, illustrates an adaptive religious landscape that resonates with Vaishnavism's core tenets and Odisha's regional cultural heritage. With its roots deeply embedded in tribal and Vedic traditions, Puri remains a sacred city revered for its enduring spiritual legacy, irrespective of the political shifts and dynastic changes that occurred around it.

The Narasimha Temple is situated on the southern side of the inner enclosure within the Jagannath Temple complex in Puri. Constructed from Baulamala and Kanda sandstone, its architectural style places it around the 10th century A.D., likely during the Somavamsi period of Odisha's history. Facing east, the temple lacks both a jagamohana and a mukhasala, consisting solely of a vimana structure, which rises to approximately 55 feet. Its plan is pancharatha, with three vertical divisions: bada, gandi, and mastaka.

Architectural Details

The square base of the vimana measures 25 feet per side, and the bada is segmented into five sections: pabhaga, talajangha, bandhana, upara jangha, and baranda. Pabhaga is intricately carved with motifs like floral designs, honeycomb patterns, and figures depicting scenes of everyday life. The tala jangha section is decorated with khakhara mundis, alasakanyas, lions, elephants, amorous couples, and figures representing the ten avatars of Vishnu, including Matsya, Kurma, Varaha, and Narasimha. The upper sections of the bada continue with elaborate motifs, including the astadikpalas, depicted seated on their respective mounts. The gandi or shikhara features a curvilinear superstructure with five pagas, each adorned with angasikharas and various ornamental designs. The mastaka includes the traditional elements of beki, amalaka, khapuri, kalasa, and chakra as the ayudha, though it lacks a dhvaja.

Deity and Iconography

The temple's presiding deity is Narasimha, enshrined in a simple simhasana. The small four-armed image, depicting Narasimha disemboweling the demon Hiranyakashyapu, holds a conch and chakra in its upper hands. The inner walls of the sanctum are plain, while the vimana's door jambs feature floral motifs and apasara figures. An image of Lakshmi-Narasimha adorns the architrave above the door lintel, though this section was partially damaged by the historical figure Kalapahada. Additionally, over sixty stone inscriptions in Sanskrit and

Oriya are present on the temple, many dating back to the reign of Chodaganga Deva (circa 1113 A.D.).

Historical and Cultural Significance

Scholars suggest the Narasimha Temple could predate the Jagannath Temple. Professor K.S. Behera compares its design to the Brahmesvara Temple, supporting a 10th- or 11th-century origin. Dr. S.N. Rajaguru posits that the temple may have initially housed the deity Purusottama in the form of Madhava before the current Jagannath Temple was built. While the Narasimha Temple's purpose and origin as a primary place of worship remain subjects of scholarly debate, many agree it likely served a role as a precursor to the Jagannath Temple's establishment.

References
- Annual Report of Indian Epigraphy, 1978-79, pp. 201-217.
- S.N. Rajaguru, Inscriptions of the Temples of Puri and Origin of Sri Purusottama Jagannatha, Vol.1, 1992.
- K.S. Behera, The Temple Complex of Lord Jagannatha at Puri, UHRJ, Vol. VI, 1995.
- J.B. Padhi, Sri Jagannatha at Puri, 2000.
- U.K. Subuddhi, The Narasimha Temple near Mukti Mandapa, in "Sri Jagannatha" Special Number, 1987

Varahi Temple

The Varahi Temple in Bali Sahi, Puri, Odisha, stands prominently near Bhandari Lane and is a significant Shakta temple dedicated to the goddess Varahi. Known for its unique architecture and tranquil atmosphere, this temple is an exquisite example of the Kalinga architectural style, specifically the Khakhara style, with rich carvings and designs emblematic of the craftsmanship of the region.

Architectural Features

The Varahi Temple is a testament to the Kalinga Kingdom's architectural legacy. The temple is constructed in the Khakhara style, characterized by a semi-cylindrical roof unique to temples associated with goddess worship in Odisha, particularly those linked to Tantric traditions. Occupying approximately two acres, the temple boasts intricate carvings, mouldings, and designs, which are regarded as remarkable examples of Kalingan art. The attention to detail seen in the exterior and interior ornamentation reflects the distinct aesthetic values of the region during the medieval period (Donaldson, 1985).

Deity: Goddess Varahi

Varahi, the principal deity, is depicted as a pot-bellied goddess with a boar's face, two arms, and a third eye on her forehead. Her iconography follows the conventions of the Sapta Matrikas, a group of seven mother goddesses frequently worshipped in tantric and Shakta traditions. She is portrayed seated on a cushion placed upon a platform, with her right foot resting on a buffalo, symbolizing her role as a powerful protector. This iconographic depiction is common across Varahi shrines and emphasizes her fearsome yet nurturing aspect.

Rituals and Offerings

The worship of Varahi is conducted through Tantric rituals. Unlike many other Hindu deities, offerings to Varahi include fish, an aspect that underscores her Tantric roots and affiliation with Shakta practices, where animal offerings are customary. These rituals are typically conducted by Tantric

practitioners and priests familiar with the esoteric aspects of the goddess's worship, adhering to specific rites and protocols meant to invoke her favor and protection.

Location and Atmosphere

The temple's proximity to the banks of the Prachi River enriches its spiritual ambiance, linking it to ancient water-based temple rituals common in Odisha. The location adds to its serene environment, which is noted for being well-maintained and relatively free from intrusive priestly practices, making it a tranquil site for devotees and visitors alike. This setting offers an atmosphere of peace and reflection, aligning with Varahi's role as a guardian deity and embodying the principles of inner peace and strength.

The Varahi Temple is not just an architectural wonder but also a spiritual haven that reflects the ancient tantric traditions of Odisha. Its architectural style, deity iconography, and ritual practices contribute to its significance within the cultural and religious landscape of Puri.

Bibliography

- Donaldson, T. E. (1985). Hindu Temple Art of Orissa. Leiden: Brill.
- Kinsley, D. (1998). Hindu Goddesses: Visions of the Divine Feminine in the Hindu Religious Tradition. University of California Press.
- Mahapatra, R. (2005). Orissa Review.

Gateswar Temple

Birapurushottampur is a quaint village, lost in anonymity until the recent attention after an ancient temple was found there. Gateswar temple is located adjacent to the newly found Swapneswar Mahadev temple. Clean and sparkling, it looked beautiful as we reached it that rainy day. The mandap where we sat waiting for the rain to stop was high and gave us a vantage point to look at the green village. The ancient shrine that has been found was also visible from there. Colourful paintings decorated the walls of the mandap while the local pundit told us stories that were not exactly old.

Every village has a place of worship for people to gather and express their devotion. Temples played a key role in villages. They were not only places of worship, but also centres for cultural and educational activities. Despite a long legacy of ancient temple architecture, temples continue to be built even today. The contemporary relevance of small temples in villages remains significant, even amid the rapid changes of modernity. These temples serve not only as spiritual centres but also play vital roles in the social and economic fabric of rural communities.

Small temples often act as focal points for community gatherings, fostering social bonds among villagers. They provide a space for cultural events, festivals, and rituals, which help maintain traditional practices and community

identity in an increasingly globalized world. Temples are repositories of local history and architecture, reflecting the artistic and cultural heritage of the region. They contribute to a sense of belonging and continuity, reminding villagers of their roots and shared values.

Many temples are beginning to embrace technology to enhance their outreach and engagement with devotees. This includes online donations, virtual tours, and digital communication platforms that connect with younger generations who may be less inclined to participate in traditional practices. Some temples are adopting sustainable practices, such as eco-friendly construction methods or promoting local crafts through fairs and exhibitions. This not only attracts eco-conscious visitors but also aligns with modern values of sustainability and community welfare.

While small temples face challenges such as declining daily participation and maintenance issues, they also present opportunities for revitalization through community engagement and innovative management practices. By empowering local communities to take charge of temple administration, these institutions can better serve their social and economic roles in contemporary society.

Small temples in villages continue to hold contemporary relevance by promoting cultural heritage, supporting local economies, adapting to modern technologies, and fostering community cohesion. Their multifaceted roles ensure that they remain integral to the identity and livelihood of rural populations amidst the pressures of modernity.

Bedhakali Temple

This temple, situated in the northwest inner enclosure of the Jagannath Temple complex in Puri, Odisha, is a remarkable yet understated architectural structure. Likely built in the 16th century, this sandstone temple is dedicated to Goddess Kali and exemplifies a blend of traditional Odishan architecture and Tantric symbolism. This chapter explores the architectural composition of the Bedhakali Temple—focusing on the vimana and mukhasala structures—and examines its possible role within the Tantric practices associated with the Jagannath temple, a known site of Shakti worship.

Located in the northwest corner of the inner enclosure of the famed Jagannath Temple complex in Puri, the Bedhakali Temple stands as a minor yet spiritually significant structure. Its presence in the complex underscores the assimilation of Tantric Shakti worship within the broader Jagannath culture. The temple is devoted to the goddess Kali, revered in Tantric traditions as a powerful manifestation of Shakti. The architectural elements and iconography of the Bedhakali Temple reflect both traditional Odishan temple design and the influence of Tantric ritual symbolism (Mishra, 1984).

Architectural Features of the Bedhakali Temple

The Bedhakali Temple is constructed with sandstone and consists of two main structures: the vimana (sanctum) and the mukhasala (porch), both facing east.

Vimana

The vimana of the Bedhakali Temple is a navaratha rekha deula (curvilinear structure) standing approximately 32 feet high. Erected on a 4-foot-high platform, its square base measures about 18 feet. The vimana consists of three distinct architectural segments: pabhaga (base), jangha (trunk), and baranda (cornice). Unlike other temples, these sections are undecorated, with no intricate carvings or iconography, a feature that may indicate its association with Tantric austerity. The central niches on three sides of the bada (base) are vacant, lending the structure an unadorned appearance (Mahatab, 1953).

The vimana's superstructure, or gandi, has nine pagas (vertical sections), thickly plastered with lime mortar, which obscures any potential decorative details. Dopichha lions, typical protective symbols in Odishan architecture, are placed atop the kanika pagas. Deula Charini figures, representing female guardians of the sanctum, are positioned at the cardinal points above the beki (neck of the tower), lending an aura of protection to the temple. The mastaka (crown) consists of a series of elements: beki, amalaka sila (ribbed disk), khapuri (skull-like cap), kalasa (vase), ayudha (symbolic weapon, here the chakra), and dhvaja (banner).

Inside the sanctum, the presiding deity, Goddess Kali, is carved in black chlorite stone. She is depicted seated, holding a khadga (sword) in her right hand and a pana patra (drinking vessel) in her left. A trefoil arch with makara (mythical sea creatures) heads frames her, underscoring her fierce aspect. The simplicity of the inner sanctum, with bare walls, may signify a space intended for focused Tantric meditation rather than elaborate ceremonial worship.

Mukhasala

The mukhasala, or entrance hall, is a pidha deula (tiered structure) with a height of about 25 feet. Like the vimana, it is built on a 4-foot-high platform, with a rectangular base measuring approximately 15 by 9 feet. The bada of the mukhasala follows a panchanga (fivefold) division typical of Odishan architecture: pabhaga, tala jangha (lower trunk), bandhana (binding element), upper jangha, and baranda. The lack of decoration on these segments aligns with the Tantric preference for unembellished structures that allow worshippers to focus on the internal spiritual journey rather than external beauty (Sharma, 2001).

The pyramidal superstructure of the mukhasala consists of two potalas (tiers), the lower containing three pidhas and the upper containing two. A jhapa simha (lion figure) decorates the eastern side of the recess between the two potalas. Dopichha lions and Deula Charini figures are similarly positioned on the mukhasala, adding a layer of protective symbolism. The mastaka features elements typical of Odishan temples, though without an ayudha or dhvaja, elements that are likely omitted to preserve the temple's Tantric austerity.

Significance of the Bedhakali Temple's Location and Tantric Link

The strategic placement of the Bedhakali Temple within the northwest corner of the Jagannath Temple complex has significant implications for its association with Tantra and Shakti worship. This position aligns with traditional Tantric cosmology, which often associates the northwest direction with protection and with fierce deities, particularly Kali (Basu, 1986). The Jagannath temple itself is well-documented as a Shakti Pitha, or sacred site of divine feminine energy, housing the temple of Vimala, the goddess who symbolizes Bhairavi, the consort of Bhairava (Jagannath) in Tantric tradition (McDaniel, 2004).

As a goddess strongly associated with Tantra, Kali's presence in the Bedhakali Temple may represent the manifestation of primal energy within the Jagannath

complex. This reinforces the view of the complex as a unified spiritual site embodying both benevolent and fierce aspects of divinity, encompassing the entire spectrum of human and cosmic consciousness. The influence of Tantra is further underscored by the simplicity of the Bedhakali Temple's architecture, mirroring the Tantric emphasis on inner devotion over external adornment (Donaldson, 1985).

Construction Date and Renovation

No historical records confirm the exact date of the Bedhakali Temple's construction, but its architectural style suggests it was built in the 16th century, consistent with other structures erected during the early medieval period in Odisha (Patnaik, 1968). Currently, the Archaeological Survey of India is overseeing renovations to preserve the temple's structure and lime-plastered exterior.

The Bedhakali Temple is a significant yet understated component of the Jagannath Temple complex. Its architectural style and Tantric symbolism reflect both the traditional Odishan temple construction, and the unique elements of Tantric worship dedicated to Kali. Its placement within the complex underscores the syncretism of the Jagannath tradition, blending Vedic, Shaiva, Shakta, and Tantric influences. The temple is a testimony to the inclusivity of Jagannath worship and the broader cultural ethos of Odisha, where diverse spiritual traditions converge in harmonious expression.

References

- Basu, S. (1986). *Tantric Visions of the Divine Feminine: The Ten Mahavidyas.* New York: Oxford University Press.
- Donaldson, T. E. (1985). *Hindu Temple Art of Orissa.* Leiden: E.J. Brill.

- Mahatab, H. K. (1953). *History of Orissa.* Bhubaneswar: Government Press.
- McDaniel, J. (2004). *Offering Flowers, Feeding Skulls: Popular Goddess Worship in West Bengal.* Oxford University Press.
- Mishra, A. C. (1984). *The Divine Presence: The Cult of Jagannath in Odisha.* New Delhi: Aryan Books International.
- Patnaik, D. (1968). *Orissan Temple Architecture.* Bhubaneswar: Government of Odisha.
- Sharma, N. (2001). *Tantric Rituals and Secret Traditions.* New Delhi: Aryan Books International.

Shyamakali Temple

Goddess Kali, a prominent figure in Hindu mythology, represents the duality of creation and destruction. In Odisha, her artistic representation is particularly significant, with a special focus on Shyamakali at Puri. This analysis delves into the historical, cultural, and artistic dimensions of Goddess Kali's portrayal in Odisha, particularly through the lens of the Shyamakali temple.

Historical Context of Goddess Kali Worship in Odisha

Odisha, situated on the eastern coast of India, boasts a rich cultural heritage characterized by its ancient temples and vibrant art forms. The worship of deities, especially Goddess Kali, is deeply embedded in the socio-religious fabric of the region. The Shyamakali temple in Puri serves as a crucial site for this worship, reflecting the historical significance of Kali within Odishan culture. The temple's origins can be traced back to the 17th century during the reign of Mukunda Deva, a king of Odisha. It was later renovated by local rulers and has since become a vital pilgrimage site for devotees seeking blessings from Shyamakali, who is revered as a benevolent form of Goddess Kali.

Artistic Representation of Goddess Kali

Goddess Kali is typically depicted as a formidable

deity with a dark complexion, adorned with a garland of skulls and wielding various weapons. Her iconography often includes multiple arms, each holding symbols that signify power and destruction. However, the representation of Shyamakali at Puri offers a unique interpretation:
- **Calm Expression**: Unlike the traditional fierce depictions of Kali, Shyamakali is portrayed with a serene demeanor.
- **Material Composition**: The idol is carved from black stone and stands approximately eight feet tall.
- **Iconographic Features**: Shyamakali is depicted with four arms; she holds a sword (khadga) in her left upper hand, a severed head in her left lower hand, and displays abhaya (fearlessness) and varada (boon-giving) mudras in her right hands.

Iconographic Details:

Feature	Description
Height	Approximately 8 feet
Material	Black stone
Pose	Stands in pratyalidha pose on Lord Shiva's chest
Attributes	Sword (khadga), severed head, abhaya mudra, varada mudra

Architectural Significance of the Shyamakali Temple

The Shyamakali temple is located near the renowned Jagannath Temple in Puri. Its architecture reflects the Kalinga style prevalent during its construction. The temple comprises several components:

- **Vimana**: The sanctum housing the idol.
- **Jagamohana**: The assembly hall for devotees.
- **Natamandapa**: A hall for dance performances.

The temple underwent significant renovations in 1957 by the Department of State Archaeology, Bhubaneswar. It features intricate carvings and paintings on its walls that depict various deities, including Durga and Shiva.

Architectural Features:
- **Construction Period**: Tentatively assigned to the 2nd half of the 17th century AD.

- **Materials Used**: Sandstones and bricks.
- **Boundary Wall**: Enclosed by a 12-foot-high wall made of bricks.

Cultural Practices and Festivals

The worship of Shyamakali is integral to various festivals celebrated in Odisha, such as Kali Puja and Durga Puja. These events attract numerous devotees who participate in rituals honoring the goddess's nurturing yet destructive nature. The temple also serves as an important cultural hub where local traditions are preserved through art and dance performances. The artistic representation of Goddess Kali in Odisha—particularly through Shyamakali at Puri—highlights a rich cultural heritage that intertwines religious devotion with artistic expression. The serene yet powerful depiction of Shyamakali emphasizes her multifaceted nature as both nurturing and fierce within Hindu spirituality. This exploration not only underscores the significance of Shyamakali but also reflects broader themes within Odishan art and culture.

References

- Tripathy, G.C. "Goddess Kali Temples at Srikshetra." *Odisha Review*, September-October 2019.
- Mohapatra, Ratnakar. "Temples of Purushottama Kshetra Puri." *Wisdom Lib*.

Leharigudi Temple

Built in the Khakhara style of architecture, this ancient shrine is in a dilapidated condition. The name of the temple could have been derived from Luipa, a tantric Siddha. Constructed on the banks of the Someswar Sagar, the temple has striking similarities with Vaital Deul of Bhubaneswar regarding style and design. Research indicates that the rudimentary temple architecture of this Sakta shrine, is indicative of a time-line close to the 5th or beginning of the 6th century A.D. Similar temple structures that are lost have left behind impressions of the glorious epoch of the area.

Its semicylindrical roof bears resemblance to the Vaital Temple of Bhubaneswar, which is part of the Dravidian Salasikhara architectural style, also known as the Kalingan Khakhara order. This architectural feature provides insight into the historical building activities of the region. The Vaital Temple is generally dated to the 6th century A.D., and it is reasonable to suggest that the Leharigudi Temple could date back to a similar or even earlier period, potentially placing its construction around the 5th century A.D. This estimation aligns with the temple's primitive architectural characteristics, which reflect an early phase of temple design typical of Sakta shrines.

The Leharigudi Temple's architecture lacks elaborate sculptural representations, a notable characteristic of early temple architecture in this style. Such a lack of ornamentation suggests that it may have been constructed during a transitional phase in temple design, possibly by the end of the 5th century or the beginning of the 6th century A.D. The Nalas, who were influential in this area until at least the 7th century A.D., likely played a role in this temple's construction and subsequent architectural developments.

Significance of Lesser-Known Temples

Lesser-known temples like Leharigudi are crucial for understanding the evolution of religious architecture in India. They often serve as indicators of regional styles and practices that may not be as well-documented as their more famous counterparts. The presence of numerous temples from various periods in Ranipur-Jharial speaks to a vibrant epoch of religious and cultural activity. These sites not only reflect architectural advancements but also provide insights into social and cultural dynamics during their time.

Temples like Leharigudi showcase early architectural

techniques that laid the groundwork for later developments in temple design. They contribute to our understanding of local traditions and practices associated with worship and community life. The deteriorating condition of such temples highlights the need for preservation efforts to protect these historical sites from further decay.

In conclusion, while the Leharigudi Temple may currently be in a deplorable state, its historical significance cannot be understated. It stands as a testament to the rich architectural heritage of ancient India and serves as a reminder of the need to preserve lesser known but culturally significant sites for future generations.

References:
- Archaeological Survey of India. Indian Archaeology – A Review. New Delhi: Archaeological Survey of India. This publication provides survey and excavation details, emphasizing the historical and architectural significance of Leharigudi Temple within the Ranipur-Jharial temple complex, reflecting its early Kalinga-style structure and religious significance.
- Sircar, D.C. (1986). Studies in the Religious Life of Ancient and Medieval India. New Delhi: Motilal Banarsidass.
- "Odishan Temples and Tantric Traditions: An Iconographic and Architectural Study," Journal of the Asiatic Society, Vol. 27, No. 4, pp. 205-225, 1985.

Someswar Temple

The group of temples at Ranipur-Jharial include few significant, monumental temples. Indralath, Chausathi Yogini and Someswara are unique for their outstanding archaeological finesse and monumental architecture. It was constructed by a famous Saiva Acharya named Gagana Siva whose inscription is found inlaid at the temple. The period of construction of Someswara Siva temple at Ranipur Jharial was the middle of the 9th century A.D. The place combined a cross section of religious faiths like Saivism, Buddhism, Vaisnivism and Tantrism. In the Somesvara temple inscription it is mentioned that "This holy place delivers (one) of all sins if one bathes here (in the tank)", People from far flung areas come here for the purpose of pindadaana.

This temple is in a good state of preservation, compared to other ruined temples in this cluster. There is an inscription by Ganganasiva, the celebrated Shaivite, here which reads *"Somasvami Siddhesvara Laxminama Chaturthanam"*. Among several images of Gods and Goddesses, there are unique images of Durga. Vrisabha, Nagi and a Dwarapala. The image of Gajalakshmi is found on the lintel of the entrance to the Garbhagriha of the temple. A distinct inscription of a deity who could be Buddha or Siddha in dhyana-mudra is found on the entrance wall and in the sanctum sanctorum, the linga symbolizing Someswar is found.

Someswar Temple, image
Source: http://ignca.gov.in/online-digital-resources

Despite its current dilapidated state, the Someswara Temple remains an active place of worship, particularly during the festival of Mahasivaratri, when it attracts large number of devotees, especially from the Saivite community. The temple is constructed on a square platform measuring approximately 12 feet 2 inches and faces east. It features a garbhagriha (sanctum) and an antarala (vestibule), both characterized by their lack of elaborate decorations or sculptures, which reflects an early architectural style.

The temple's structure is massive, with heavy, plain pillars and pilasters that contribute to its robust appearance. The overall design follows a Trirath style, comprising three vertical sections: bada, gandi, and mastaka. The bada includes a shallow right-angle projection for the pabhaga (base), while the jangha (middle section) is devoid of decorative elements. The gandi is curvilinear yet plain, adding to the temple's austere aesthetic. Inside the garbhagriha, there is a Sivalinga alongside a copper snake. The doorway is adorned with sculptural panels, including a prominent figure of Gajalaxmi on the lintel. An inscription on the door lintel details four deities: Some (Shiva), Swami (Kartikeya), Siddheswara (Buddha), and Lakshmi, with Someswara as the presiding deity.

Someswar Temple, image
Source: http://ignca.gov.in/online-digital-resources

The temple serves as a vital centre for Saivite worship in the region and attracts not only devotees but also archaeologists and architecture enthusiasts due to its unique characteristics and historical context. While many temples in the vicinity are in various states of disrepair, Someswara Temple continues to draw attention for its enduring spiritual relevance and architectural integrity. The Someswara Temple at Ranipur-Jharial exemplifies early medieval Indian temple architecture, showcasing both simplicity and grandeur in its design. As an active place of worship steeped in history, it represents an essential link to understanding the cultural and religious landscape of ancient Odisha. Its continued use highlights not only its architectural merits but also its role in sustaining community identity through religious practices. The temple stands as a testament to the rich heritage of temple architecture in India, warranting further study and preservation efforts to ensure that its legacy endures for future generations.

Lankeswari Temple

The Lankeswari Temple, located in the picturesque Sonepur town of Subarnapur district, Odisha, is renowned for its stunning natural beauty and is considered a unique tourist destination. Nestled along the banks of the Mahanadi River, this delightful shrine attracts visitors not only for its spiritual significance but also for its scenic surroundings. Historically, the Sonepur region was known as Paschima Lanka, with Goddess Lankeswari revered as the presiding deity. The temple holds cultural importance for the local Kaivarta (fisherman) community and the broader population of Subarnapur district. The area's historical ties to the legendary King Ravana of Lanka further enrich its narrative; it is believed that Ravana brought the goddess to Sonepur due to his military presence in the region. This connection has led to Sonepur being referred to by various names, including Swarnapuri Lanka and Dwitiya Lanka, reflecting its stronghold in Tantric and Shakti culture.

Originally, a rock was worshiped as the deity at this site; however, a structured temple has since been constructed. The temple is situated near a deep gorge known as Lankeswari Darha, which offers breathtaking views of both the river and the town. The temple's architecture is simple yet striking, harmonizing with its natural environment. Visitors can engage in activities such as sailing and fishing in Lankeswari Darha, providing a unique opportunity to

connect with local fishermen and experience the region's aquatic life first-hand. This interaction not only enhances the visitor experience but also supports local traditions and livelihoods.

The Lankeswari Temple serves as a focal point for community worship and cultural practices in the region. The goddess is venerated during various festivals, drawing large crowds who partake in rituals and celebrations that reflect the area's rich cultural heritage. The temple's continued relevance underscores its role in fostering community identity and spiritual devotion among locals.

The Lankeswari Temple stands as a testament to Odisha's rich cultural tapestry, intertwining history, spirituality, and natural beauty. As one of the unique tourist destinations in Subarnapur district, it offers visitors not only a glimpse into ancient traditions but also an opportunity to experience the serene beauty of the Mahanadi River. The temple's significance extends beyond its architectural features; it embodies the enduring spirit of the local community and their connection to their heritage. Further research and preservation efforts are essential to maintain this cultural landmark for future generations while promoting sustainable tourism in the region.

Temples Of Mahendragiri

Mahendragiri Hills, located in the Gajapati District of Odisha, India, are a significant geographical and cultural landmark. These hills rise majestically, offering a panoramic view of the surrounding landscape and hold a rich historical legacy tied to ancient temple architecture and local legends. The region is not only known for its natural beauty but also for its archaeological significance, with several ancient temples that reflect the architectural styles of different periods. The Mahendragiri Hills serve as a crucial link between the past and present, embodying the socio-religious dynamics of the area.

Rising majestically at an altitude of around 1,500 meters, these hills are steeped in mythology, ancient temple architecture, and legends associated with the Mahabharata. Believed to be a favored retreat for the Pandava brothers during their exile, Mahendragiri holds a cluster of temples named after the Pandavas, which showcase ancient and unique architectural styles that highlight the historical legacy of Odisha. The scenic beauty of Mahendragiri, combined with its rich heritage, makes it an attractive destination for trekkers, historians, and pilgrims alike. Below is a brief overview of the key temples on Mahendragiri Hill.

Bhima Temple

The Bhima Temple, the smallest and oldest on

Mahendragiri, sits at the highest local peak, Kubjagiri, around a kilometer away from the Yudhisthira Temple on a lower peak. Reaching the Bhima Temple requires ascending a narrow, winding pathway, but the temple is visible from the Yudhisthira Temple area. Although there are no historical records confirming the name "Bhima," it is well-known by this title. The temple structure stands approximately 7 meters high with a square layout of around 4 x 4 meters, built from about 26 massive stone blocks. These blocks, each about 3 x 3 meters, form a one-chambered *Rekha Deul* style structure. The temple lacks intricate sculptures but is marked by a *beki* (narrow band) followed by an *amalaka* (stone disc) on top, aligning it with the early Odishan style. Scholars believe that it was originally a flat-roofed structure and potentially reconstructed with the addition of an *amalaka* stone. Archaeologists speculate its construction could date back to the Mathara King Uma Varmana (360-395 CE), aligning it with the Gupta period and linking it to early examples of Kalinga architecture.

Yudhisthira Temple

Positioned lower on a flat area of the Mahendragiri peak, the Yudhisthira Temple is widely recognized and dedicated to Shiva. The temple represents a tri-ratha style with a single-chamber structure that rises straight from the ground and features a pointed projection with an *amalaka* on top. The entrance, facing south and standing about six feet high, is adorned by four *chaitya* arches on the *sikhara* (tower) and enclosed by a boundary wall of large stone slabs. This temple closely resembles the Satrughanesvara group of temples in Bhubaneswar, dating to the late 6th or early 7th century CE. Despite lacking intricate artwork, the temple's tri-ratha design aligns it with other early Odishan temples, reflecting the region's evolving architectural forms. Some scholars suggest that the current temple was rebuilt over an original structure, and an inscription by the Chola king Rajendra Chola has been found on its front door lintel.

Gokarnesvara Temple

Known locally as the Kunti Temple, the Gokarnesvara Temple is further east from the Yudhisthira Temple, on another flat area of the hill. Dedicated to Gokarnesvara

Shiva, it is referenced in several copper plate charters and features a single-chambered shrine with the *Rekha Deul* style. Standing approximately 30 feet tall, the temple has no plinth and faces west. The square sanctum houses a Shiva linga, and the niches contain representations of Parsvadevatas (side deities). The narrow doorways, flat roof, and squat *sikhara* with a fluted *amalaka* indicate its transitional period from Gupta to Post-Gupta architecture. Although some sculptures, such as the Ganesha and Karttikeya, are well-preserved, others, like the Parvati figure on the north side, are severely damaged. Inscriptions found on the lintel and nearby stones suggest a construction period around the 9th-10th century CE, with repairs and restorations over time. K.C. Panigrahi noted the temple as one of Odisha's oldest, frequently cited in the records of the Ganga dynasty.

Cultural and Historical Significance of Mahendragiri Temples

These temples on Mahendragiri Hills form part of a socio-religious network, connecting the local people with their cultural roots. Each temple serves as a spiritual gateway, embodying Hinduism's divine symbols and mythology. Scholars suggest that the temples were built in such a remote, rugged terrain by the Eastern Gangas, who integrated local deities like Gokarnesvara into mainstream worship, eventually unified under the Jagannath cult.

Mahendragiri's location near the coast and ancient ports such as Palur and Kalingapatnam suggests its historical significance as a trade route hub, connecting northern and southern India. Evidence of the Chola king Rajendra Chola's inscription further underlines Mahendragiri's strategic importance. Additionally, the association with ancient Hindu-Buddhist cultural exchanges between India and Southeast Asia highlights the region's influence beyond Indian borders.

Today, Mahendragiri is a rich historical site and a potential eco-heritage tourism destination, ideal for trekkers, art enthusiasts, and history lovers. The hills represent a blend of natural beauty, mythological connections, and architectural heritage, providing a unique opportunity for promoting cultural tourism and creating sustainable economic opportunities for the local communities.

References
- Mathur, S.M., *Physical Geography of India*, NBT, 2003.
- Ratha, B.K., "The History of Mount Mahendra," *Odisha Historical Research Journal*, Vol. XXII.
- Behera, S.C., *Rise and Fall of Sailodbhavas*, Punthi Pustak, Calcutta, 1982.
- Kulke, H., *Kings and Cult*, Manohar, Delhi, 2001.

Murga Mahadev Temple

The temple is nestled at the foothills of Thakurani Hills, Keonjhar, Odisha amidst the lush greenery of the forest and a perennial spring. It is a popular tourist spot, and devotees gather here during Makara Sankranti and Shivaratri. Situated around 70 km away from Keonjhar town, it is an ancient place of worship. The word Murga Mahadev originated from two words Murugan and Mahadev, denoting Kartikeya and Shiva respectively in Dravidian languages. Historians opine that it is an ancient place of worship of tribal gods which later converted to place of worship for Hindus. I had vivid recollection of the temple from our visits almost twenty years back. In all this time, the temple had retained its anonymity though few structures have been built.

Murga Mahadev Temple, nestled in the scenic Keonjhar district of Odisha, India, is an important pilgrimage site dedicated to Lord Shiva. Located near the Kanjhari Dam and surrounded by a lush, serene landscape, the temple attracts both devotees and tourists alike. Known for its spiritual significance and picturesque environment, Murga Mahadev has become a centre for worship and cultural activities in the region. Murga Mahadev Temple is steeped in local mythology and folklore, and it holds special significance for Shiva devotees. The name "Murga

Mahadev" is derived from local languages, representing the deity Mahadev (Shiva) in a form revered by the indigenous communities. The temple is particularly significant for the tribal and rural communities of Keonjhar, who hold it in high esteem as a place of divine blessings and auspicious rituals.

The architecture of Murga Mahadev Temple is modest and traditional, reflecting the simple yet profound devotion of the people in the area. Although it is not a grand or elaborate structure like many other historical temples in Odisha, its simplicity adds to its charm. The temple is situated amidst thick forests, enhancing its natural beauty and providing a tranquil atmosphere conducive to meditation and worship.

Throughout the year, the temple is a venue for various religious activities and rituals dedicated to Lord Shiva. Among these, the most prominent is the celebration of Maha Shivaratri, which attracts large crowds from surrounding areas. During this festival, devotees undertake fasting, prayers, and night vigils in honor of Lord Shiva. Many

visitors also perform "Jala Abhisheka" (water offerings) and seek blessings for their well-being and prosperity.

Located near the Kanjhari Dam and surrounded by forests and hills, the temple's setting provides a peaceful retreat for visitors. The area around Murga Mahadev is popular for trekking, picnics, and nature walks, making it a destination that combines spiritual experience with nature tourism. Murga Mahadev Temple in Keonjhar represents a beautiful confluence of spirituality, local culture, and nature. With its scenic surroundings, simple architecture, and significant cultural value, the temple serves as a peaceful sanctuary for worshippers and a cherished site within Odisha's spiritual landscape.

Tantra Temples

Land of the Sacred Feminine

Odisha, known in ancient times as *Uddiyan*, has long held a prominent position in the field of tantra throughout India. Tantric practices, a spiritual system that combines ritual, meditation, and symbolism, found fertile ground in Odisha, thanks in part to influential figures such as King Indrabhuti and his sister, Princess Laksmikara. Indrabhuti, a king of Sambalpur of Utkal or Udra-desha was a Boudha-tantric with deep belief in the Vaisnab's deity, Lord Sri Jagannath. His deep devotion is reflected in his writings of verses in 'Jnyana-sidhi' book.

As tantra gained popularity, numerous tantric centres emerged across Odisha, with Bhubaneswar emerging as a prominent hub. Known as *Ekamrakshetra* in texts like the *Ekamrapurana, Svarnadri Mahodaya, Kapila Samhita, Ekamrachandrika*, and *Tirtha Cintamani* by Vachaspati Mishra, Bhubaneswar became a key site for tantric practices. These texts reveal the ancient designation of Bhubaneswar as a sacred site dedicated to Lord Shiva, also known as *Krutibasakshetra*, further supporting the city's significance as a Sakta (Shakti) tantric *peetha* (sacred centre).

The Lingaraj Temple: A Saiva Tantric Peetha

One of the foremost tantric sites in Bhubaneswar is

the Lingaraj Temple, a sacred *Saiva Peetha* (centre of Shiva worship). Here, the unique western-facing *linga* (symbol of Shiva) is an example of tantric symbolism, as this orientation aligns with tantric teachings in the *Tantra Shastra*. The rituals associated with Lingaraj are deeply tantric, with specific mantras like *Om Hrim Hroom Sankara Narayanaya Namah Haroom Hrim Om* used during worship. This illustrates the intertwining of Saivism and tantric traditions in the region.

There has been significant syncretism observed in Odisha too. The Vaishnava and Shaiva streams have

often flown side by side as typified by the twin temples of Gandharadi in Boudh. In Lingaraj both tulsi and bel leaves are offered to the Lord and the symbol atop the temple is half a trident along with half a wheel symbolising the intimate co-existence of Shaivism with Vaisnavism. Predating this multifaceted spirituality, runs the tradition of the worship of the Sacred Feminine from which ensues Tantric lore and practices which have found their way into Hinduism, Jainism and Buddhism as a common thread and vibration incorporated into all these three major religions. For example the same Goddess Varahi in Chaurasi have been part of the Jaina, Hindu and Buddhist tradition in different times.

The Lingaraj temple is surrounded by various deities, including a north-facing, two-armed Ganesha statue, located on the temple's left side, believed to embody tantric qualities. Additionally, Kapali Peetha and Parasurameswar Temple are worth noting for their tantric features, such as the figure of Goddess Dakshina Kali in the south of the temple, worshipped in the *Bhairava* (fierce) form, characteristic of tantric worship.

Bhubaneswari and Other Tantric Deities of Bhubaneswar

Beyond Lingaraj, another prominent deity associated with tantric worship in Bhubaneswar is Bhubaneswari, the presiding goddess of *Ekamra* (another name for Bhubaneswar). Her worship, often conducted alongside that of Lord Lingaraj, reinforces her standing as a central figure in the region's tantric practices. Surrounding the Lingaraj temple are various *Peethas* (sacred sites) representing different aspects or forms of Lord Shiva. Known collectively as *Astamurtti*, these include deities like Ganesh, Devi (goddess), Skanda (Kartikeya), and others.

Historians have often held the view that the worship of the goddess preceded the worship of the present main deities in both Puri and Bhubaneswar temples. The Tantra and Shakta ways have also predated the advent of Vedic worship, aryanisation and sanskritisation.

Sacred Waters and Temples Around Bhubaneswar

In the vicinity of Lingaraj lies *Bindu Sarovara* (Bindu Tank), encircled by eight *chandi* (tantric goddesses) who are collectively known as *Astachandi*. These goddesses include *Sukapola* and *Kapali Devi* in the west, *Mohini* and *Bindhyabasini* in the south, *Uttarayani* in the north, and *Dvarabasini* and *Ambika* in the east. Other significant sites around Bindu Sarovara include Siva Gauri Temple at *Siddhasram*, reinforcing the significance of Bhubaneswar as a major tantric site. The influence of *Shakti* (goddess) worship can be observed in the temple sculptures across Bhubaneswar, especially with representations of the *Saptamatrika* (seven mother goddesses), which date back to early times. The *Vaital* or *Kapalini* Temple, an 8th-century structure, houses an inner sanctuary dedicated to the fierce deity Chamunda, signifying the early and intense practice of Shakti worship in the area.

From the numerous tantric relics and inscriptions found throughout Bhubaneswar, it is evident that the region has been a historic centre for Saivism and Shaktism, closely intertwined through tantric practices. Dr K.C. Panigrahi suggests that the erotic sculptures seen on temple walls may reflect the influence of Tantrikas and Kapalikas, who held unique philosophical views on life, the body, and spiritual power. Together, these findings establish Bhubaneswar as a significant tantric centre in Odisha.

Western Odisha holds a significant place in India's

tantric tradition, known for its diverse Sakta (Shakta) peethas, or sacred centres dedicated to the worship of goddess energy. Odisha, and particularly its western region, has long been a focal point of tantric practices, where devotion to the goddess (Shakti) manifests in various forms and local deities. Historical records and inscriptions point to a long-standing Sakta tantric tradition in Odisha, especially within the medieval kingdoms that spanned Dakshina Kosala (present-day western Odisha and parts of Chhattisgarh). This tradition thrived in royal courts, village shrines, and tantric peethas, integrating elements from non-Aryan tribal worship and mainstream Hinduism. Scholars such as A. Antemen and Hermann Kulke have noted that Sakta worship during this period often blended with tribal animism, exemplified by the integration of deities such as Khambesvari (Stambesvari) and Samalesvari, who retain pre-Aryan characteristics even within the tantric framework.

Sakta Tantric Centres of Western Odisha
Khambeswari (Stambesvari) Peetha

The Khambesvari (or Stambesvari) peetha, believed to have been established around the 5th century A.D, is one of the oldest centres of Tantra in western Odisha. Often depicted as a pillar or stambha, the goddess Khambesvari represents a bridge between tribal animistic practices and Sakta tantra. German scholar A. Antemen identified Khambesvari with the deity Subhadra from the Jagannath tradition of Puri, suggesting a shared worship pattern. The Khambesvari peetha reflects early tantric practices, where the goddess was venerated using rituals involving yantras (sacred geometric diagrams) and bija mantras (seed syllables), characteristic of Sakta tantra.

Samaleswari Temple

The temple of Samalesvari, located near the city of Sambalpur, is dedicated to the goddess Samalei (or Samaleswari), who is venerated as a powerful tantric deity. The iconography of Samaleswari includes weapons and a fearsome visage, resonating with other Sakta deities associated with power and protection. At this temple, offerings typically include fish and meat, aligning with tantric rituals that emphasize symbolic transgression and devotion to fierce forms of the goddess.

Temples at Sonepur

There are many temples in Sonepur, an ancient seat of civilisation of Odisha, where the worship of Goddess in tantric tradition is alive. The worship of Lankeswari, Sureswari, Metakani etc which indicate the strong tantric roots and rituals prevalent there. The lore of the seven sadhikas like Nitei Dhobani, Pitei Sauruni ,Gyanadei

Maluni etc were doing their sadhana in Sonepur. Odisha has been witness to cult of the sacred feminine and women empowerment and gender symmetry in spirituality. It also highlights the democratic temper of religion in Odisha

Dwaraseni Temple

The Dwaraseni Peetha, located in the village of Sindhekela in Balangir district, is among the most unique Sakta tantric centres of western Odisha. Here, a yoni symbol, locally called "Badan," represents the feminine creative power. According to oral tradition, the tantric rituals of Dwaraseni incorporate Gautamiya Tantra techniques, which are believed to bring spiritual fulfilment and protection. The goddess Dwaraseni is worshipped as Mahadurga, with Lal Kishore Chandra Deo, a prominent worshipper, emphasizing the use of tantric mantras in her rituals.

Other Notable Deities and Practices

Western Odisha's Sakta traditions include numerous deities whose origins trace back to tribal and animistic roots, predating Aryan influence. Non-Aryan deities like Pitavalli, Maulli, Ghasien, and Dvaraseni are still venerated in village shrines, reflecting the cultural continuity of Odisha's early tantric traditions. The goddess Patanesvari, considered a form of Durga, is one such deity deeply embedded in the history of the Chouhan dynasty, whose kings adopted her as their family deity.

The Kosalesvara Siva temple near the Patanesvari temple demonstrates the close association between Saivism and Shaktism, particularly in the integration of goddess worship within Siva-centric practices. In Patnagarh, formerly the capital of Dakshina Kosala, seven female practitioners, or *kumaris*, were trained in tantric rituals by Brahmanaguru Dhanantvari, exemplifying the importance of feminine energy in Sakta traditions. Known figures like Jnanadei Maluni, one of the *kumaris* and author of *Sashisena Kavya*, reflect the strong cultural role of women in Odisha's tantric practices.

Iconography and Rituals

The iconography of western Odisha's Sakta temples displays a range of tantric symbolism, such as the four-armed Mahesvari standing in the *abhaya mudra* (gesture of fearlessness), often featured in ancient sculptural representations. Other prominent icons include the twelve deities of Samalesvari, with names like Mahakali, Chinnamasta, Varahi, and Ugratara, embodying various aspects of the goddess and illustrating the multiplicity of forms in Sakta worship.

These deities are venerated through complex rituals involving yantras, offerings of fish, meat, and alcoholic drinks, and the recitation of bija mantras. Such practices underscore the transgressive nature of Sakta tantra, where offerings and rituals deviate from mainstream Hindu norms to embody Shakti's transformative power. Western Odisha's Sakta tantric centres reflect a distinctive blend of Aryan and tribal elements, creating a unique regional tradition within the broader context of Indian tantra. These Peethas continue to serve as vital cultural and spiritual centres, preserving the essence of Sakta tantra as practiced in medieval Odisha. Further research into these traditions can deepen our understanding of the region's religious history and the ways in which Sakta tantra has influenced local customs, iconography, and belief systems.

The spiritual culture of Odisha signifies great syncretism and inclusivity while retaining a mystic touch and artistic aura.

References
- Antemen, A., & Kulke, H. (1989). *The Cult of Stambesvari in Ancient Odisha.* Berlin: De Gruyter.
- Eschmann, A., & Kulke, H. (1978). *The Cult of Jagannath and the Regional Tradition of Orissa.* New Delhi: Manohar.
- Panigrahi, K.C. (1961). *Archaeological Remains at Bhubaneswar.* New Delhi: Government of India.
- Panda, B. (2017). "Tantric Centres of Western Odisha." *Odisha Review,* ISSN 0970-8669
- Krutibasavidham Ksetra: Excerpt from the Skanda Purana, Maheswari Khanda, Sloka 38.
- Tatrastau Candika: Odishara Tantra Samskruti.
- Archaeological Remains at Bhubaneswar by Dr. K.C. Panigrahi.
- Odishara Tantra Samskruti by Dr. Balaram Panda.

Black Eagle Books

www.blackeaglebooks.org
info@blackeaglebooks.org

Black Eagle Books, an independent publisher, was founded as a nonprofit organization in April, 2019. It is our mission to connect and engage the Indian diaspora and the world at large with the best of works of world literature published on a collaborative platform, with special emphasis on foregrounding Contemporary Classics and New Writing.

www.ingramcontent.com/pod-product-compliance
Lightning Source LLC
Chambersburg PA
CBHW060608080526
44585CB00013B/735